Chronology

Silhouetted against the early morning sky, Matildas of 7 RTR attack the Sidi Barrani perimeter on 10 December 1940. (Imperial War Museum—as are all photographs not specifically credited elsewhere)

June 1940

Italy declares war on Great Britain (10th). 7th Armoured Division begins harassing operations against Italians along Egyptian-Libyan border (11th); during next three months the British inflict more than 3,000 casualties, and suffer 150.

September 1940

Italians invade Egypt (13th); they reach Sidi Barrani (18th) and halt to consolidate with chain of fortified camps.

December 1940

Operation 'Compass' (9th): 7th Armd.Div. isolates Sidi Barrani; 4th Indian Div., spearheaded by 7th Royal Tank Regiment, storms camps at Nibeiwa, Tummar West, Tummar Central and Tummar East. 4th Indian Div. and 7 RTR storm Sidi Barrani (10th). Italians abandon Rabia, Sofafi camps and withdraw towards frontier (11th). 7th Armd.Div. pursue; action with rearguard at Buq-Buq (12th).

January 1941

6th Australian Div. and 7 RTR storm Bardia (3rd–5th), Tobruk (21st–22nd). Italians abandon defence line based on Wadi Derna, withdraw through Benghazi (28th).

February 1941

7th Armd.Div. cuts across 'Benghazi Bulge', blocks Italian retreat at Beda Fomm (5th); Italians attempt to break through without success; 6th Australian Div. closes in from north, entering Benghazi (6th). Italian army surrenders (7th).

February–March, increased Luftwaffe activity over N. Africa; advance elements of Rommel's Afrika Korps arrive in Tripolitania.

March 1941

Rommel attacks, breaking through British at El Agheila to cut across Benghazi Bulge (24th).

April 1941

Benghazi, Msus evacuated (4th); fragmented 2nd Armd. Div. beaten in detail and never re-formed (5th–6th); Gen. Sir Richard O'Connor captured, Derna falls (7th). 9th Australian Div. encircled in Tobruk (13th); German attack repulsed (14th). Rommel takes Halfaya Pass on Egyptian frontier (25th) and captures Sollum (28th). Axis domination of frontier zone complete.

May 1941

Operation 'Brevity' (15th): Halfaya, Sollum temporarily recaptured, but operation fails elsewhere.

8th Hussars Mk VIB, its multiple pennants identifying a navigator's tank—see sun compass bracket. Some units preferred this method to the more conventional blue or long black flag, as being less obvious to the enemy; these pennants may be in green/black/green, with the top one in yellow unit seniority colour.

June 1941

Operation 'Battleaxe' (15th–17th): British repulsed at Halfaya and Sollum, but take Fort Capuzzo. In south, 7th Armd. Bde. drive towards Tobruk blunted, and weakened by mechanical problems of Cruiser tanks. British successfully disengage, withdraw into Egypt. Each side loses approx. 100 tanks, but DAK able to recover most of theirs.

July 1941

Gen. Wavell, unfairly blamed for failures in Greece and during 'Battleaxe', replaced by Gen. Sir Claude Auchinleck as C-in-C Middle East (1st).

November 1941

Operation 'Crusader', to relieve Tobruk and destroy Axis in Libya, begins (18th). British armour comprises 7th Armd.Div. with three armd.bdes.—4th, 7th, 22nd—in 30 Corps; 1st Army Tank Bde. supporting 13 Corps on coast; and 32nd Army Tank Bde. leading Tobruk garrison break-out. 22nd Armd.Bde. fights Italian *Ariete* Armd.Div. inconclusively near Bir el Gubi (19th). 'Multi-layer' tank battle develops SE of Sidi Rezegh, leaving British armour weakened and in confusion (21st–23rd); but Tobruk garrison consolidates gains. Rommel attempts to provoke withdrawal by raid into British rear— 'the Dash to the Wire' (24th); but British com-

British Operational Code Names		
'Aberdeen'	...	8th Army's attack on the Cauldron, 4/5 June 1942
'Battleaxe'	...	Wavell's attempt to relieve Tobruk, June 1941
'Brevity'	... ...	Attempt to regain control of Egyptian frontier zone, May 1941
'Bulimba'	... ...	Australian attack with Valentine tank support, Sept. 1942.
'Compass'	... ...	Attack on Italian positions at Sidi Barrani, Dec. 1940
'Crusader'	... ...	Relief of Tobruk and recovery of Cyrenaica, Nov.–Dec. 1941
'Fullsize'	... ...	50th Div. and 1st Armd. Div. attack under 13 Corps, 18/19 March 1942, to neutralise Axis airfields as Malta convoy passes; 8 RTR and dummy tank units involved
'Lightfoot'	...	Opening phase of Second Alamein, October 1942
'Manhood'	...	30 Corps attack using elements of 23rd Arm.Bde. and 'A' Force deception units, 26 July 1942
'Sentinel'	... ...	Deception scheme to create impression of large Aug./ Sept. 1942 reinforcements in rear of hard-pressed 8th Army
'Sinbad'	... ...	'A' Force deception operation to test Axis strength in Bir Tegender area, 29–30 April 1942
'Splendour'	...	13 Corps attack, 22 July 1942
'Supercharge'	...	Break-out phase of Second Alamein, Nov. 1942

mand refuses to panic and uses respite to reorganise. Led by 44 RTR in brilliant night attack, 2nd NZ Div. links up with Tobruk garrison (26th). Alarmed, Rommel returns from frontier (27th); Axis troops are gradually forced to abandon rest of their siege perimeter (27th–5th Dec.).

VANGUARD SERIES

EDITOR: MARTIN WINDROW

BRITISH TANKS
in N. AFRICA
1940-42

Text by

BRYAN PERRETT

Colour plates by

PETER SARSON and TONY BRYAN

OSPREY PUBLISHING LONDON

Published in 1981 by
Osprey Publishing Ltd
Member company of the George Philip Group
12–14 Long Acre, London WC2E 9LP
© Copyright 1981 Osprey Publishing Ltd

ISBN 0 85045 421 2

Filmset in Great Britain
Printed in Hong Kong

Acknowledgements
The author and publishers are grateful for the
assistance of Col. P. W. H. Whiteley, OBE, TD;
and of George Balin, Simon Dunstan, C. O. Ellis,
David List and the late John Sandars.

Select Bibliography
Wavell's Offensive, Bryan Perrett, Ian Allen Ltd
Tobruk, Michael Carver, Pan
El Alamein, Michael Carver, Pan
Alamein, C. E. Lucas Phillips, Pan
Crucible of Power—the Fight for Tunisia, Kenneth
    Macksey, Hutchinson
*Through Mud and Blood—Infantry Tank Operations in
    World War II*, Bryan Perrett, Robert Hale Ltd
The Mediterranean and the Middle East, Vols I-IV,
    Playfair & Molony, HMSO
The Camouflage Story, G. Barkas, Cassell
Deception in World War II, C. Cruikshank, OUP
Master of Deception, D. Mure, William Kimber

December 1941

Severe losses and supply difficulties oblige Rommel to withdraw from Cyrenaica, and conduct fighting withdrawal to El Agheila (6th–30th). Bardia stormed by 2nd South African Div., 8 and 44 RTR in support (31st).

January 1942

Axis garrison at Halfaya surrender (17th). 'Crusader' has cost Axis 300 tanks and British 278—but many of latter are recoverable. Reinforced, Rommel attacks anew (21st), breaking through outpost line at El Agheila, moving through Msus, and outflanking Benghazi, which falls (29th).

February 1942

8th Army stabilises line at Gazala (5th). Both sides prepare for fresh offensive for four months.

May 1942

Panzerarmee Afrika wheels round southern end of Gazala line at Bir Hacheim (26th–27th), but is brought to standstill after heavy fighting with 1st Armd.Div.—2nd, 22nd Armd.Bdes.—and 4th Armd.Bde. of 7th Armd.Div.; Rommel is forced onto defensive, with his back against British minefields. Lt.Gen. Ritchie, GOC 8th Army, fails to take concerted action against Rommel's 'Cauldron' position (28th–4th June), which is strengthened. Rommel overwhelms 150th Bde. Box across his rear, almost destroying 1st Army

Light tanks Mks VIA and VIB photographed in August 1940. Spotlights were standard on the tanks of 1 and 6 RTR; and one tank from each squadron of the 6th was lent to 7th Hussars for a night attack on Fort Capuzzo on 29/30 June 1940, two of them using their lights to dazzle and confuse Italian gunners.

Tank Bde. in process (31st).

June 1942

Attacks on Cauldron by 22nd Armd.Bde. from east and 32nd Army Tank Bde. from north repulsed with heavy loss; enemy counter-attack overruns 10th Indian Inf.Bde. (5th). Ritchie fails to co-ordinate adequate relief operations for besieged Free French Box at Bir Hacheim (6th–10th); French break out successfully (10th). Rommel renews his original NE thrust, inflicting serious tank losses on British in actions around 'Knightsbridge' track junction (11th–13th). Ritchie orders retreat into Egypt, prepares Tobruk for second siege. Tobruk stormed and surrenders (20th), with loss of 2nd SA Div., 201st Guards Bde., 11th Indian Inf.Bde., and two of the Royal Armoured Corps' finest regiments, 4 and 7 RTR. British morale reaches lowest ebb; 8th Army continues retreat to Mersa Matruh, and Auchinleck assumes personal command (21st–25th). Rommel, maintaining close pursuit with handful of tanks, penetrates gap between British 10 and 13 Corps, causing disorderly withdrawal from Mersa Matruh to El Alamein (26th). 6 and 8

5

Before the arrival of the Diamond-T Transporter the recovery of untowable 'dead' tanks was more difficult. This A9 is being hauled on to a light trailer for 'back-loading'; the striped bar on the turret may identify a navigator's tank.

RTR destroy 20 of Italian *Littorio* Div.'s 30 tanks at Bir el Tamr—a significant check, given total Axis tank strength of approx. 50 (30th).

July 1942

Start of series of engagements known as '1st Battle of Alamein'; 1st Armd.Div. checks DAK's advance (1st). 1st Battle of Ruweisat Ridge (14th–15th): heavy fighting at Tel el Eisa; Alamein line consolidated. 2nd Battle of Ruweisat Ridge (22nd)—Operation 'Splendour': 23rd Armd.Bde. lose 93 of 104 tanks. Both sides reach limit of their resources as 1st Battle of Alamein ends.

August 1942

Gen. Sir Harold Alexander replaces Auchinleck as C-in-C Middle East (13th); Lt.Gen. Bernard Montgomery assumes command of 8th Army. Battle of Alam Halfa (31st–7th September): Rommel attempts to repeat movement which had won him 'Knightsbridge', but his anticipated advance is slowed by 7th Armd.Div., and stopped by 10th Armd.Div.—8th, 22nd and 23rd Armd. Bdes. DAK withdraws behind its own lines.

October 1942

2nd Battle of Alamein begins—Operation 'Lightfoot' (23rd). Attempted break-through by 7th and 10th Armd.Divs. stalled by Axis defence (24th–25th). 1st Armd.Div. in heavy fighting at Kidney Ridge (26th–27th). 23rd Armd.Bde. continues to support infantry 'crumbling' attacks on northern sector (28th–30th). 40 RTR repulse counter-attack on 9th Australian Div. at Thompson's Post (31st).

November 1942

Operation 'Supercharge': 7th Armd. and 2nd NZ Divs. break through (2nd–3rd); Rommel begins withdrawal. Axis casualties total approx. 59,000 men, 500 tanks, 400 guns; 8th Army casualties approx. 13,000 men, and 432 tanks disabled. Pursuit delayed by fuel shortage and heavy rain (5th–7th). (Operation 'Torch'—landing of Anglo-American 1st Army in French North Africa—takes place on the 8th. New arrivals include 6th Armd.Div., with 26th Armd. Bde.; and 21st and 25th Tank Bdes.) 8th Army enters Bardia (11th), Tobruk (13th), Benghazi (20th).

December 1942

Rommel withdraws from El Agheila 'bottleneck' (13th); 8th Army reaches Sirte (21st). Logistic problems reduce the Army to 30 Corps during advance through Tripolitania: 7th Armd.Div., 2nd NZ Div., and 51st Highland Div., with 23rd Armd.Bde.

January 1943

8th Army breaks through Axis position at Buerat (16th); occupies Homs (19th); enters Tripoli (23rd).

February 1943

On the 4th, 8th Army reaches the Tunisian frontier.

★   ★   ★

It seems logical to set a period to this book at this point, the character of, and to some extent the units and tanks involved in, the Tunisian campaign being so different from the 'classic' desert period as to require a separate book.

A9, believed to be in use by the Italian 63rd Tank Bn. in 1940. It may be T.3536 of 'A' Sqn., 1 RTR, abandoned on 14 September 1940 when its tracks were blown off by artillery fire, and removed by Italian forces. Later Intelligence reports suggested that the Italians were using a Cruiser to penetrate night leaguers by deception; and as late as July 1942, HQ 2nd Bn., 27th Inf.Regt., *Pavia* Div. was reported to have a British tank and an armoured car on strength. Whether these were all the same tank is, of course, open to conjecture; but the Italians were not in a position to capture many British tanks. (Martin Windrow)

The Desert War

For many Britons, particularly among the older generations, the campaign in North Africa has a nostalgic appeal, and indeed a glamour, which has never been associated with the fighting in Italy, North-West Europe and Burma. The reasons are largely emotional but entirely understandable, as for three years it constituted the only lasting contact between the British and Commonwealth armies and those of the Axis powers. Again, there is a long British tradition of wars fought successfully in the remoter areas of the globe and, however many setbacks might be encountered along the way, this was accompanied by a justified national confidence in eventual victory.

As the years have passed so too have generalisations about the campaign multiplied; and although such generalisations may contain a core of truth, they do bear examination. Most commonly heard among detractors is the complaint that Britain was forced to deploy a high percentage of her available strength in the area, whereas Germany employed only a handful of divisions. This fails to take into account the fact that the Commander-in-Chief Middle East was also required to mount simultaneous operations over a vast area including Persia, Iraq, Syria, Eritrea, Ethiopia and Somaliland; and that on two occasions, when victory seemed to be within his grasp, he was forced to send very substantial reinforcements to other theatres. Thus, having utterly routed the Italian army at Beda Fomm in February 1941, Wavell was immediately required to send troops to Greece; while in December of that year, with Rommel still retiring from the 'Crusader' battlefield, Auchinleck was ordered to strip his command of some of his best formations and send them to counter the Japanese offensive in the Far East. Neither does this view admit that in spite of committing most of her strength to this theatre as well, Italy was virtually knocked out of the Axis alliance; nor the fact that had Germany employed *more* good-quality troops, and above all kept them properly supplied, she might have produced a result more favourable to herself—as it was, OKW favoured a limited involvement which tied down numerous British divisions in defence of the Middle East's vital oil-producing areas when they would otherwise have been preparing for a return to the mainland of Europe.

Many, too, hold the attractive but simplistic view that an immediate advance on Tripoli after the victory of Beda Fomm would have ended the campaign in early 1941. Wavell had destroyed the Italian field army and turned Cyrenaica into a buffer zone; in view of the urgent orders to reinforce Greece, Tripoli was an irrelevance. While Gen. O'Connor believed that captured stores would have enabled him to reach Tripoli, there seemed at the time no reason for such a march. Few could have foreseen the outcome of Rommel's first bold probing attack, described by Halder, Chief of the German General Staff, as the action of 'a dangerous lunatic'.

Although the British Army had, over the years, acquired as much desert experience as any other, the fact remained that in 1940 no one had fought a fully mechanised desert campaign, and few knew what to expect. That the British were initially better prepared than the Italians is a tribute to the demanding exercises instituted by Maj.Gen. Percy Hobart, commander in 1939 of the Mobile Division Egypt—later, 7th Armoured Division. As the Italians became more mechanised they too learned to operate in the desert; and the Germans adapted to it very quickly. Apart from such special units as the Long Range Desert Group, there was in the end little to choose between the desert-craft of the different armies. There was, however, one important flaw in the British philosophy, which cursed the conduct of armoured operations for fully a year.

In his *Tobruk* Field-Marshal Lord Carver analyses the disastrous defeat in the Gazala/Knightsbridge battles and mentions, *inter alia*, the indirect influence of Lawrence of Arabia. Regarded in the inter-war years as the fount of all desert wisdom, and specifically endorsed in 1935

Some armour was shipped to the Middle East still in UK livery, with unmodified radios, engines and filters and required tropicalising. Here HMS *York* looms behind A10s and A13s of 2 RTR, newly landed in October 1940, still in 3rd Armd.Bde. markings with BEF '0046' mobilisation serials. 2 RTR and 3rd Hussars were rushed out to reinforce 7th Armd.Div. for Operation 'Compass'.

even by Liddell Hart, Lawrence's writings stressed the analogy of desert warfare as resembling sea warfare. Mobility, independence of bases, the ignoring of fixed directions and strategic areas, fluidity, dispersal, mystification of the enemy—these were the themes developed by Lawrence, the supreme 'Irregular'. But the desert armies of the Second World War were organised and trained along strictly Regular lines, and the philosophy of the virtually self-sufficient camel-raid served them ill. The Deutsches Afrika Korps did not practice dispersion, and although it suffered occasionally from the consequent vulnerability to air attack, its concentration all too often made it the stronger contestant at the point of contact. Those British commanders who formed their judgements in the light of historical precedent found Allenby a more rewarding source than Lawrence.

Two further generalisations were that the desert war was 'a tactician's paradise and a quartermaster's hell'. The first is only partly valid. While there were areas of hard, level going, the desert also contained a wide variety of landscapes limiting to the freedom of mechanised forces: treacherous salt marshes, deep wadis, boulder fields, shifting dunes, and the ancient sea cliffs which formed escarpments. Certain areas were of prime importance: El Alamein, where the Qattara Depression and the coast cut the available frontage to 40 miles; Halfaya Pass and Sollum, which provided a means of climbing the escarpment from the coastal plain; and the deep-water harbour of Tobruk, possession of which eased the logistic burdens of either side. It was in these areas that the majority of the decisive fighting took place. Particularly significant was the Benghazi Bulge; British possession of its airfields allowed convoys to run through the Mediterranean Narrows to Malta, but the Bulge was easily vulnerable to outflanking via the cross-country route Agedabia-Msus-Mechili, and was untenable in itself.

As for the desert being a quartermaster's hell, this may well understate the case. The integrity of mechanised armies was totally dependent on a huge consumption of water and fuel. In launching his reluctant invasion of Egypt in 1940 with an essentially *marching* infantry army, Graziani pre-

Radio silence was a frequent tactical necessity; here a troop leader resorts to semaphoring the signal 'Advance'. Note sun compass platform on right.

dicted that a desert defeat would rapidly escalate into a disaster, and so it transpired: beaten at Sidi Barrani, tens of thousands of Italians surrendered rather than endure the horrors of a waterless retreat.

Logistics were of even greater importance in the desert than in other theatres of war. Each side operated from distant bases, and since fuel is a self-consuming load, the further they advanced the less reached them. Victorious armies had their advances terminated as much by supply difficulties as by enemy action; conversely, the closer an army retreated to its source of supply, the more troops it was able to maintain in the field. After Alamein Montgomery could only pursue the enemy with a fraction of the forces that had fought in that battle, and then only by stripping the transport from the formations left behind. After the fall of Tobruk Rommel could advance deep into Egypt only by virtue of captured stores, and captured transport to move them.

Lack of fuel haunted armoured commanders of both sides. The Royal Navy's sinking of a critical Axis supply convoy on the night of 8/9 November 1941 forced Rommel to abandon a major attack on Tobruk and seriously inhibited his conduct of the later stages of the 'Crusader' fighting.

A13 Mk IIs photographed in August 1941. Visible are differing mantlet patterns, a steel helmet used as a headlight cover (right), and a small squadron mark on the turret front (centre)—possibly indicating 2nd Armd.Div., who authorised this practice.

Further naval and air interference left his tanks so short of fuel at Alamein that he strove to avoid a mobile battle which must inevitably lead to the destruction of the DAK. Seeing this, Montgomery embarked on a 'crumbling' offensive, attacking first in one place and then in another, so forcing the Panzers of Rommel's counter-attack force to burn up precious fuel as they moved up and down the front.

The cause of British fuel shortages was insidious rather than dramatic. In contrast to the robust German 'jerrycans', British fuel was shipped forward in tins that were aptly nicknamed 'flimsies'. Unequal not merely to rough handling but even to the inevitable jostling of supply trucks, they frequently burst at the seams and leaked their contents into the sand. Eventually they were replaced by a direct copy of the jerrycan.

The attitudes of the combatants has led to the campaign being described as 'the last of the gentlemen's wars', and at the outset a certain *fin de siécle* professional courtesy was not unknown. It was initially considered bad form to shoot up a crew escaping from a stricken tank; but before long both sides recognised that trained men were harder to replace than tanks. There were isolated incidents of which neither army had any reason to feel proud; but by and large, once the heat of battle had cooled, each side treated its prisoners very fairly. There was no love lost between them, but rather a mutual respect for men who could stand up to the harsh demands of desert fighting.

For the desert was cruel, and impartial. In the searing heat of noon it was impossible to touch the metal of a tank; in the freezing nights a man might shiver, sleepless, even though he wore every stitch he possessed. There were sandstorms which might last for days. With careful management a man might save enough of his water ration for a cursory wash and shave; nonetheless, after some days in the field it became possible to recognise a companion in the dark by his smell. The desert was far from sterile. Despite strict codes of hygiene, the human waste of large armies inevitably attracted flies in their millions, which swarmed maddeningly around leaguer areas, spreading their filth, until movement or a *kham-*

seen brought temporary relief. Most men suffered from desert sores. The inevitable small cuts and grazes were invaded by dirt and flies, and were painful and slow to heal.

The enforced celibacy was also a trial. In more hospitable climes the British Army, traditionally puritanical, prescribed Cold Showers and Healthy Sport as a panacea for disturbing thoughts. In the desert such remedies were impractical; consequently, formations returning to the Delta or Cairo for rest tended to go hard for the professional ladies of Egypt. The more open-minded Axis armies maintained field bordellos, and one of these establishments actually succeeded in delaying 8th Army's advance on Tripoli. As they stormed along the coast road 40 RTR came across its staff waiting angrily by the roadside, their transport having been appropriated by their last customers to expedite their own escape. As the regiment paused to comfort these unhappy women, Authority roared up the column to put a stop to the party: the encounter was not, in his opinion, of such importance as to justify a temporary halt in the North African campaign.

In the end it is the shared experience and the comradeship which are remembered. The 8th Army had a personality all its own, and its style and dash were reflected in its vehicles, its dress and even its speech. Those who served in it are justifiably proud of the fact.

Clear study of an A13 of 2 RTR shortly after arrival in Egypt, with straight-edged 'Caunter' camouflage and ID pennants added.

The Tanks

For space reasons, the following notes omit detail of vehicles covered separately in other titles in this series: the M3 Stuart ('Honey'), in Vanguard No. 17, the M3 Lee/Grant in Vanguard No. 6, the Churchill in Vanguard No. 13, and the M4 Sherman in Vanguard No. 15.

During the pre-war years it had been believed that the Royal Armoured Corps[1] would require three classes of tank: the Light, for Imperial policing, reconnaissance, and to equip divisional cavalry regiments of infantry divisions; Cruisers, the principal equipment of the armoured divisions; and Infantry tanks, heavily armoured to support infantry assaults on fortified positions. By 1939 all three had been under development for some time, although Infantry tanks were not present in Egypt at the outbreak of war with Italy in 1940.

Light tanks

Engine 66hp Rolls-Royce, Mks II, III; 88hp Meadows subsequent Marks. *Protection* 14mm max. *Armament* 1 × .303 or .50 MG (Mks II-IV), 1 × .303 plus 1 × .50 (V, VI), 1 × 7.92mm plus 1 × 15mm MGs (VIC). *Crew* Commander/gunner, driver (Mks II-IV); commander, gunner, driver (V, VI). *Max. speed* 35mph.

Very fast, but so thinly armoured that they were vulnerable to small-calibre AP weapons and even near-misses by HE shells, the Mks II-VI served in the desert. The Light tanks performed their reconnaissance rôle adequately, and were at their best beating up supply convoys; although capable of defeating the wretched Italian CV-33s —little better than tracked MG carriers—they had no other place in the tank battle. It was maliciously hinted by RTR officers that their cavalry colleagues felt at home in the vehicle due to its distinctly equine motion; if driven too fast it suffered 'reversed steering', an unnerving and self-explanatory phenomenon. Decreasing numbers served until late 1941.

[1]Created shortly before the war, the RAC incorporated the cavalry and the RTR. Pre-war, each considered the other a threat to its continued existence; the mutual hostility of 1939 disappeared in the shared experience of battle, though separate traditions were preserved.

Cruiser tanks
Mk I (A9)

Eng. 150hp AEC. *Prot.* 14mm max. *Arm.* 1 × 2-pdr., 1 × .303 MG, water-cooled, co-axial; 2 × .303 in subsidiary forward turrets. *Crew* Commander, loader/operator, gunner, driver, plus two hull gunners if MG turrets manned. *Weight* 12 tons. *Max. speed* 25mph.

Originally classed as a Medium to replace the Vickers Medium, the A9 employed the Vickers 'slow motion' suspension. Crew shortages often led to the subsidiary turrets being used only as stowage space. 125 vehicles built. The last A9s to see action fought in Operation 'Crusader'.

Mk II (A10)

Eng. & *susp.* As A9. *Prot.* 30mm max. *Arm.* 1 × 2-pdr., 1 × .303, water-cooled, co-ax.; Mk IIA, co-ax. MG changed to 7.92mm air-cooled Besa, plus second Besa, hull front. *Crew* C, L/O, G, D; plus hull G in Mk IIA. *Wt.* $13\frac{3}{4}$ tons. *Max. speed* 15mph.

Designed as Infantry tank version of A9, with subsidiary turrets removed and 30mm frontal armour; 175 examples were built, the last being withdrawn from service at the end of 1941. Although classified as a Heavy Cruiser it was too slow for the rôle, and by 1940 its armour was too thin to allow effective infantry support; the A10 thus fell unhappily between two stools. A few were converted to Close Support tanks by substitution of a 3.7in. howitzer for the 2-pdr.

Mk IV (A13)

Eng. 340hp Nuffield Liberty. *Prot.* 30mm max. *Arm.* 1 × 2-pdr., 1 × .303, water-cooled, co-ax.; Mk IVA, co-ax. MG changed to 7.92mm air-cooled Besa. *Crew* C, L/O, G, D. *Wt.* $14\frac{3}{44}$ tons. *Max. speed* 30mph.

From Mk III onwards British Cruisers adopted the Christie suspension, demonstrated successfully by BT types on Russia's 1936 manoeuvres. The Mk III, apart from the Nuffield Liberty engine and Christie suspension, was very similar to the A10; it did not serve in the desert, but led directly to the A13 which did. The latter had sharply angled and undercut turret sides giving a degree of spaced-armour protection; some 335 were built, the last being withdrawn after Operation

'Crusader' and sent to Cyprus to equip units of 25 Corps' island defence 'Crusader Force'.

Mk V, Covenanter
Eng. 300hp Meadows. *Prot.* 40mm max. *Arm.* 1 × 2-pdr., 1 × 7.92mm Besa co-ax. *Crew* C, L/O, G, D. *Wt.* 18 tons. *Max. speed* 31mph.

Over 1,700 were built, but only a handful went to the Middle East, probably limited to training; photos of examples in forward areas may possibly suggest some use in action, if orders of battle included them under the similar 2-pdr. Crusader. The engine cooling system gave problems in this theatre. A logical development of the A13, the Covenanter had a more streamlined turret through better use of angled plate.

Mk VI, Crusader (A15)
Eng. 340hp Nuffield Liberty. *Prot.* 40mm max. (Mk I), 49mm (Mk II), 51mm (Mk III). *Arm.* 1 × 2-pdr., 1 × 7.92mm Besa co-ax., 1 × 7.92mm

Crusader I, T.43744, photographed at an Egyptian base camp. (RAC Tank Museum)

Inside Tobruk, September 1941: an A9 crew of 1 RTR cast off camouflage netting and prepare for action. Forward subturrets were often unmanned, due to manpower shortages; and the desperate need for AA weapons in the Tobruk perimeter led to at least one MG being removed from each tank for the purpose.

Besa in subsidiary turret (Mk I, part run Mk II); 1 × 6-pdr., 1 × Besa co-ax. (Mk III). *Crew* C, L/O, G, D, plus hull G if subsidiary turret manned. *Wt.* 19 tons (Mks I, II), $19\frac{3}{4}$ tons (Mk III). *Max. speed* 27mph.

Its five large road wheels and sleekly angled

British Armoured Order of Battle
Second Battle of El Alamein
23 October 1942

Army Troops

8th Army HQ
  Protection Sqn. ... 7 × Grant, plus
                      armoured cars
1st Army Tank
  Brigade ... ... 12 × Matilda Scorpions
                      crewed by 42 &
                      44 RTR

74th Armoured Bde. of 'A' Force, forming
  'Melting Force'
39th, 118th & 124th
Royal Tank
Regiment ... ... Dummy tanks

10 Corps
(Lt.Gen. Herbert Lumsden)
Corps HQ ... ... 2 × Crusader 2-pdr.

1st Armoured Division
(Maj.Gen. Raymond Briggs)
Divisional HQ... ... 8 × Crusader 2-pdr.
12th Lancers ... ... Armoured cars
'Kingforce' ... ... 6 × Churchill Mk III
                    6-pdr.

2nd Armoured Bde.

The Queen's	1 × Grant,
Bays	92 × Sherman,
9th Lancers	38 × Crusader 2-pdr.,
10th Hussars	29 × Crusader 6-pdr.

10th Armoured Division
(Maj.Gen. A. H. Gatehouse)
Divisional HQ... ... 7 × Crusader 2-pdr.
The Royal Dragoons Armoured cars

8th Armoured Bde.

3rd Royal Tank Regiment	57 × Grant,
Sherwood Foresters Yeomanry	31 × Sherman,
Staffordshire Yeomanry	33 × Crusader 2-pdr., 12 × Crusader 6-pdr.

24th Armoured Bde.

41st Royal Tank Regiment	2 × Grant,
45th Royal Tank Regiment	93 × Sherman, 28 × Crusader 2-pdr.,
47th Royal Tank Regiment	17 × Crusader 6-pdr.

13 Corps
(Lt.Gen. B. G. Horrocks)
7th Armoured Division
(Maj.Gen. A. F. Harding)
Divisional HQ... ... 7 × Crusader 2-pdr.

The Household Cavalry Regiment	
11th Hussars	Armoured cars
2nd Derbyshire Yeomanry	

---

turret made the Crusader one of the most aesthetically satisfactory tank designs ever built. Originally conceived as a Heavy Cruiser, in fact a further projection of the A13/Covenanter theme, its speed made it a very difficult target—and the Christie suspension allowed speed across the desert as well as on metalled roads. Eventually it became popular with its crews, but initially it was a mine of trouble; the original air filter was inadequate for the desert and quickly clogged, the fan drive frequently broke, and the gear selector was unreliable. At one stage more Crusaders were being lost through breakdown than enemy action—although the inadequate armour also failed to resist the DAK's anti-tank guns. 5,300 Crusaders were built; their first actions in the desert were fought with 6 RTR in June 1941 during Operation 'Battleaxe', and thereafter they served throughout the campaign, declining in relative importance with the arrival of the American Mediums. A number were converted to Close Support tanks by substitution of a 3in. howitzer.

Infantry tanks
Mk II, Matilda (A12)
Eng. 174 combined hp twin AEC diesels. *Prot.* 78mm max. *Arm.* 1 × 2-pdr., 1 × 7.92mm Besa co-ax.; 3in. howitzer in CS version. *Crew* C, L/O, G, D. *Wt.* $26\frac{1}{2}$ tons. *Max. speed* 15mph.

4th Light Armoured Bde.

4th/8th Hussars
The Royal Scots Greys ⎫ ... ... 14 × Grant,
67 × Stuart

22nd Armoured Bde.

1st Royal Tank Regiment
5th Royal Tank Regiment
4th County of London Yeomanry ⎫ 57 × Grant,
19 × Stuart,
42 × Crusader 2-pdr.,
8 × Crusader 6-pdr.

30 Corps
(Lt.Gen. Oliver Leese)

9th Armoured Bde.

3rd King's Own Hussars
Royal Wiltshire Yeomanry
Warwickshire Yeomanry ⎫ ... 37 × Grant,
36 × Sherman,
37 × Crusader 2-pdr.,
12 × Crusader 6-pdr.

23rd Armoured Bde.

8th Royal Tank Regiment
40th Royal Tank Regiment
46th Royal Tank Regiment
50th Royal Tank Regiment ⎫ ... 194 × Valentine 2-pdr.

2nd New Zealand Divisional Cavalry Regiment ... ... 29 × Stuart
9th Australian Divisional Cavalry Regiment ... ... 15 × Crusader 2-pdr.,
4 × Stuart

Thus, excluding Scorpions, 8th Army's first-line strength in gun tanks totalled 1,035, with a further 200 of various types in immediate reserve, and approximately 1,000 more undergoing repair or modification in workshops and 'coming on stream'. Less than 10 per cent of the Crusader 2-pdrs. were Close Support models.

Self-propelled artillery was also present in the shape of the new American M7 Priest 105mm Howitzer Motor Carriage, and the British 25-pdr. Bishop based on the Valentine chassis, both equipments serving in the RA regiments within armoured formations.

In the infantry-heavy 30 Corps the 9th Armoured Bde. operated under command of 2nd NZ Division; 23rd Armoured Bde., under Brig. G. W. Richards, was the Corps Infantry Tank formation and was engaged during the battle under 1st SA, 2nd NZ, 9th Australian and 51st Highland Divisions.

The armament of the Matilda was conventional, and for its Infantry rôle its speed was governed down to a very modest figure; but its 78mm frontal armour rendered it impervious to Italian and initial DAK weapons, and during Operation 'Compass' and its sequel it earned the title 'Queen of the Battlefield' in the hands of 7 RTR. The DAK urgently requested *Panzerjäger* equipment to deal with the threat (see Vanguard No. 12, *Sturmartillerie and Panzerjäger*). Its dominance was ended by the appearance of the dual-purpose German 88mm gun during Operation 'Battleaxe', but it remained a formidable opponent for another year and was largely responsible for the relief of Tobruk. Steering clutches wore out quickly, however, and the turret ring area was vulnerable to jamming by shell splinters. Suffering severely in the Gazala/Knightsbridge battles, Matilda ended its desert service converted to Scorpion mine-flails at Second Alamein.

Mk III, Valentine
Eng. 135hp AEC petrol (Mk I); subsequently, 131hp AEC diesel or 138hp GMC diesel. *Prot.* 65mm max. *Arm.* 1 × 2-pdr. (Mks I-VII); 1 × 7.92mm Besa co-ax. (Mks I-V); 1 × 7.92mm Browning co-ax. (Mks VI, VII—which were Canadian built, and almost all sent to the USSR); 1 × 6-pdr. without co-ax. MG (Mks VIII, IX). *Crew* C/L, G/O, D; (Mks III, V) C, L/O, G, D.

Wt. 16–17 tons. *Max. speed* 15mph.

This Vickers Armstrong Ltd. private venture was accepted as a mass-production supplement to the Matilda in 1939; over 8,000 were built, representing 25 per cent of Britain's entire tank production, and after North Africa many were converted to a variety of special rôles. It employed the 'slow-motion' suspension which had proved itself on the A9 and A10; and was a by-word for reliability—by the time 40 RTR reached Tunisia some of its tanks were still going strong after 3,000-plus operational miles. The two-man turret crew was a disadvantage rectified, by cramped internal re-arrangement, on the Mks III and V. Although armament was as inadequate as in all other British tanks of the period, the diminutive size of the Valentine—height 7ft. $5\frac{1}{2}$ins.—allowed it to obtain a good hull-down position in any convenient fold in the ground. Valentine first saw action with 8 RTR in Operation 'Crusader', and subsequently fought throughout the campaign, a few 6-pdr.-armed models arriving in time for the Tunisian campaign.

Mk IV, Churchill (A22)

Eng. 350hp Bedford. *Prot.* 102mm max. *Arm.* 1 × 6-pdr., 1 × 7.92mm Besa co-ax., 1 × Besa in hull front. *Crew* C, L/O, G, D, hull G. *Wt.* 39 tons. *Max. speed* $12\frac{1}{2}$mph.

These figures relate to the Mk III Churchill, of which six fought under direct command of 1st Armoured Div. HQ in an experimental unit, 'Kingforce', at Second Alamein. For details of this and subsequent Tunisian service by this very successful tank, see Vanguard No. 13.

American tanks

Light Tank M3, Stuart

For full details of use in North Africa and technical description, see Vanguard No. 17. The Stuart's mechanical reliability, and refusal to shed tracks whatever the provocation, together with a 36mph top speed, earned it the heart-felt nickname 'Honey'. With 37mm frontal armour,

Crusader II of HQ, 'C' Sqn., 6 RTR prior to Operation 'Crusader'. 'F-names' adorned many of the battalion's tanks below the squadron mark—e.g. 'Ferocious'. Netting and tank 'bivvy' sheets are strapped front and rear. A cloth squadron commander's pennant flies above tin ID pennants —a common replacement for cloth ones, which quickly became tattered. (RAC Tank Museum).

a 37mm gun and a weight of $13\frac{1}{2}$ tons it had more in common with British Cruiser than Light tanks, and its first major desert battle was in 'Crusader', when it equipped three regiments of 4th Armoured Brigade (8th KRIH, 3 and 5 RTR). It served on for the rest of the campaign, generally limited to regimental Light squadrons and recce troops.

Medium Tank M3, Lee/Grant

For full details of use in North Africa and technical description, see Vanguard No. 6. The sponson-mounted 75mm main armament of these tanks, the 340hp–375hp engines, and the 65mm armour gave 8th Army a chance to meet the DAK Panzers on something like equal terms at last; but the unsound layout prevented hull-down firing. First in action in the Gazala/Knightsbridge battles with 4th Armoured Brigade, the M3 series remained 8th Army's main battle tank at First Alamein and Alam Halfa; it fought at Second Alamein, although by then the Sherman had begun to overshadow its importance, and a few survivors reached Tunisia.

Medium Tank M4, Sherman

The mainstay of British armoured divisions from

November 1941: a Matilda with extra sand-bag protection, possibly flying the blue battalion commander's flag with white number of 4 RTR below the 'two top, blue' pennants ordered as ID by 32nd Army Tank Bde. for 'Crusader'.

Second Alamein onwards, the Sherman is described in detail in Vanguard No. 15. At 30 tons, with 76mm frontal armour and a conventionally turret-mounted 75mm gun, the Sherman put 8th Army crews on almost an equal footing with the DAK. Its presence in numbers at Second Alamein was partly due to President Roosevelt's entirely characteristic generosity in stripping his own incomplete 1st Armored Division as replacements for part of the first North African shipment which had been lost at sea. The cast-hull M4A1 (Sherman II) was the most common 8th Army type, but the welded-hull M4 and M4A2 (Shermans I and III respectively, the latter diesel-engined) were also used.

Armament

The only tank gun to serve throughout the campaign was the 2-pdr., which was an adequate weapon for the first year of the war, just acceptable for the second, and hopelessly out-ranged for the third. It would have been replaced by the 6-pdr. much earlier had not the BEF lost so much

7 RTR refuel, replenish ammunition and repair minor damage at a 'Forward Rally' during the Sidi Barrani operations of December 1940; the broken track (right) is mine damage.

equipment at Dunkirk, the subsequent invasion scare leaving factories no time to re-tool. By the time the 6-pdr. entered service it was still a match for the German 50mm L/42, but was quickly overtaken by the 50mm L/60. The American 75mm gun provided a temporary weapon superiority, although this soon disappeared when the Germans began fitting their PzKpfw IV with the 75mm L/48 gun. Fortunately these vehicles were never sufficiently numerous to affect the overall position, and the 88mm-armed Tiger was only encountered in small numbers in Tunisia.

At this period the 2-pdr. and the 6-pdr. fired only armour-piercing shot, and could not reply effectively to anti-tank guns, which usually outranged them. Because of this the Close Support tank was developed, armed with a 3in. howitzer which fired a high-explosive shell, and one or two tanks of this type operated under the control of squadron headquarters. This was a less satisfactory solution to the problem than that practised by the Panzerwaffe, who, until 1942, maintained an entire company of 75mm L/24 howitzer PzKpfw IVs as part of the Panzer battalion establishment. The American 75mm gun, firing both AP and HE, placed British crews in a much happier position when confronted with an anti-tank gun screen.

However, the uncomfortable feeling of being out-gunned was to haunt the Royal Armoured Corps throughout the campaign and beyond, and the fact was that the Germans were much quicker to get larger weapons into their tanks, spurred on by their experiences on the Eastern Front. (See also Vanguard Nos. 16, *The Panzerkampfwagen III*, 18, *The Panzerkampfwagen IV*, and 20, *The Tiger Tanks*.) German optical equipment, including gun sights, was also superior to British and American. A high percentage of British losses were, however, caused by *Panzerjäger* and anti-tank guns rather than in tank-v-tank fighting, and although many of these were put down to the dreaded '88', the 50mm and 75mm anti-tank guns, well sited, could be just as deadly.

Organisation and Method

The Armoured Divisions

When Operation 'Compass' was mounted, the 7th Armoured Division consisted of two armoured brigades, each of three armoured regiments and an anti-tank battery; a Support Group which included a field artillery regiment and two motorised infantry battalions; and divisional troops including an armoured car regiment, an anti-tank/anti-aircraft regiment, and Royal Engineer and logistic support units.[1] The armoured brigades were equipped with Light tanks and Cruisers A9, A10 and A13. As the campaign progressed the composition of these changed and the divisional commander, Major-General O'Moore Creagh, insisted that each regiment should contain at least one Cruiser squadron—3rd Hussars and 2 RTR accomplished this by exchanging B Squadrons, including personnel, respective regimental equipment being Lights and Cruisers. The Support Group was deployed by the divisional commander as a pivot of manoeuvre which could provide fire support for the armoured brigades' missions and could also form a rallying point.

The 7th Armoured Division's basic organisation had apparently changed little for Operation 'Battleaxe', although the nature of the operation has been misunderstood. The plan called for 7th

Armoured Brigade (2 RTR with A9s, A10s and A13s and 6 RTR with Crusaders) to work its way round the southern flank of the Axis frontier defences and advance towards Tobruk. Simultaneously the 4th Indian Division with 4th Armoured Brigade (4 and 7 RTR, both Matilda regiments) *under command*, would storm those defences at Halfaya Pass, Sollum and Fort Capuzzo. In theory, the infantry would then release 4th Armoured Brigade, which would then revert to the control of 7th Armoured Division, but, in the event, neither wing of the offensive was successful. That part of the latter was equipped with Matildas was not, as has been stated elsewhere, because 'nothing else was available'; these objectives were strongly fortified and it was considered, rightly, that only heavily armoured Infantry tanks could suppress them. Again, since more than one regiment was employed, an intermediate brigade headquarters was necessary,

[1]For the full order of battle see Vanguard No. 1, *7th Armoured Division 1940–45.*

By March 1942 the overstriping had generally given way to overall Light Stone, and this Matilda, T.17723, has areas of UK green paint visible on the front 'horns' showing where the sandshields have been removed.

Shipped from the UK in 1942 as the War Cabinet's 'floating option', for commitment to Australia if Japan invaded or for Middle East reinforcements, 8th Armd.Div. was pre-painted in tropical colours and had some markings obliterated. Landing at Suez in July, 23rd Armd.Bde. was hurriedly prepared for action; for the sake of speed many tanks were taken over from 24th Armd.Bde., whose personnel were still at sea. This 40 RTR Valentine unloading from a Z-Lighter follows common regimental practice in being named after a warship—'Mohawk'; the div. sign is overpainted. See also Plate E1.

and that was supplied by HQ 4th Armoured Brigade, which was otherwise unemployed.

During 'Crusader' the 7th Armoured Division was roughly the size of a Panzer corps. It deployed no less than nine armoured regiments organised in three armoured brigades, the 4th with Stuarts, the 7th with Crusaders and older Cruisers, and the 22nd with Crusaders; the 4th was actually a Brigade Group, and incorporated an artillery regiment and a motorised infantry battalion. The Support Group contained two 25-pdr. regiments, an anti-tank regiment and two infantry battalions. Divisional troops included three armoured car regiments, an anti-tank regiment, an anti-aircraft regiment, and logistic services. This organisation was too unwieldy for a single divisional headquarters to control satisfactorily, and was difficult to administer; nor was the formation a balanced one, having too much armour in proportion to the available artillery and infantry.

These defects were duly noted in the 1942 reorganisation of the British armoured division,

under which the number of armoured brigades was reduced to one, consisting of three armoured regiments and a motorised infantry battalion. The Support Group disappeared and the second armoured brigade was replaced by a three-battalion motorised infantry brigade. Divisional troops included an armoured car regiment, four 25-pdr. regiments (one of which might be attached on a semi-permanent basis to the armoured brigade), an anti-tank regiment, an anti-aircraft regiment, and divisional services.

However, while this basic structure was adopted by armoured divisions in both the 1st and 8th Armies, several were given a second armoured brigade at various periods in their careers. Thus at Gazala, while 7th Armoured Division had one armoured brigade (the 4th), 1st Armoured Division had two (the 2nd and 22nd); and at Second Alamein the 1st Armoured Division had one (the 2nd), while the 7th Armoured Division had two (the 4th Light and the 22nd), as did the 10th Armoured Division (the 8th and 24th). An independent armoured brigade, the 9th, was attached to the 2nd New Zealand Division during the battle.[1]

The internal organisation of the armoured regiment varied only in detail throughout the campaign and consisted of three fighting squadrons, a headquarters squadron incorporating the supply echelon and other administrative elements, and a reconnaissance troop of scout cars which operated under regimental control. In action the regiment was commanded from a three-tank Regimental Headquarters Troop. Squadrons were organised with four troops, each of three or four tanks, and a Squadron Headquarters Troop, usually of three. In squadrons equipped with 2-pdr. and 6-pdr. tanks, one or two SHQ vehicles would be Close Support models.

Given this structure, regiments were further organised according to their equipment. Mention has already been made of the integration of Light and Cruiser tanks during Wavell's offensive, and a similar process was followed when the better-armed Grants and Shermans began entering

[1]7th Armoured Brigade, the original Desert Rats, left the Middle East after 'Crusader' to earn fresh laurels in Burma. See Vanguard No. 17, *The Stuart Light Tank Series*.

service. At Gazala the three regiments of 4th Armoured Brigade (8th Hussars, 3 RTR and 5 RTR) each had two Heavy squadrons of Grants and one Light squadron of Stuarts. At this time the regiments of 2nd Armoured Brigade (The Queen's Bays, 9th Lancers and 10th Hussars) and 22nd Armoured Brigade (2nd Royal Gloucestershire Hussars, 3rd and 4th County of London Yeomanry) each had one Grant Heavy squadron and two Light squadrons armed with Crusaders. During Second Alamein regiments strove to maintain two Heavy squadrons equipped with Shermans and Grants, and one Light squadron with Crusaders or Stuarts; the exceptions were the two regiments comprising 4th Light Armoured Brigade, whose equipment is described elsewhere.

The rôle of the armoured divisions was defined loosely as exploitation, although there was also a general acceptance of Fuller's principles of deep penetration and the benefits to be gained by using the indirect approach. These were applied brilliantly by O'Connor at Sidi Barrani in December 1940 and again at Beda Fomm in February 1941; interestingly, O'Connor had studied neither Fuller nor Liddell Hart and later described his tactics as being merely those of common sense. After his capture in the spring of 1941 his sure touch on the helm was sorely missed.

Something of the debilitating effect of dispersion tactics has already been mentioned. These actually had their roots in O'Connor's period of command when the grossly outnumbered British were forced to stretch their forces thin and to rely on mobility to retain the initiative over the Italians. Small columns, consisting perhaps of a lorried infantry battalion, a squadron of armoured cars and a troop each of field and anti-tank guns, harried the Italians without respite and attained a complete moral ascendancy. After Graziani's army had been eliminated the need for

8 RTR Valentines dispersed over the desert near Bardia during Operation 'Crusader', January 1942; note the partially obliterated red/white/red flashes.

Diamond-T of No. 1 Tank Transporter Coy. RASC lifts a 50 RTR Valentine to the forward area, July 1942. The yellow 'strong man and tank' was the company insignia. Both vehicles are overall Light Stone. Valentine T.17644 carries the number on nose and sides, a large 'C' Sqn. circle, the unit serial '67' and an overpainted 8th Armd.Div. sign.; note jettison fuel tank.

such dispersed units, called 'Jock Columns' after their originator Brig. Jock Campbell of the 7th Armoured Division Support Group, disappeared. Notwithstanding, the entirely understandable urge to be 'off the leash' and to prolong the *beau sabreur* aspect of the war led to their continuance long after they had ceased to produce an economic return for the effort expended. The worst aspect of the Jock Columns was that their existence diluted the strength of the divisional artillery just when it was needed most to deal with the anti-tank gun aspect of the Panzer divisions' sword-and-shield tactics.

Dispersion was also practised within the armoured division itself. It took far longer and cost far more than had been anticipated to achieve success in 'Crusader', and in part the reason lay in that 7th Armoured Division's three armoured

brigades were deployed too far apart to be able to support each other when the need arose. As Rommel commented to a prisoner, 'What difference does it make if you have two tanks to my one, when you spread them out and let me smash them in detail? You presented me with three armoured brigades in succession.'

The fault was far from being cured at Gazala, and was indeed compounded by a thoroughly unsatisfactory relationship between the army commander and his two corps commanders, which led to debate when decision was required and to temporisation when action was needed. It was ironic that in this battle, in which the British for once decisively out-gunned their opponents, they should suffer their worst defeat. Significantly, the tank crews knew exactly what was wrong and also its cure; a soldier of 5 RTR wrote to his family, 'It seemed to me that if they [i.e. his generals] had got a lot of kit together and had one big push in one place, we could have done something definite. As it was, the units were just battering themselves to pieces in a lot of little scraps which were getting us nowhere.'

Rommel's dashing style of forward control has sometimes been cited as a contrast to the 'bumble-dom' affecting the British army command at this period of the war. In fact it merely provided a contrast in inefficiencies. Rommel was frequently out of contact with his staff and unaware of crucial developments, was supremely lucky to avoid capture on several occasions, and was rescued from disaster by his opponent's mistakes. Nonetheless, the long British retreat to Alamein was made with the sickening smell of defeat hanging over the 8th Army, and a feeling that Rommel always seemed to be just one jump ahead. A certain staleness was inevitable, accompanied by an unhealthy cynicism. In addition, it had always been slightly resented by the Com-monwealth troops that *all* the armoured formations were British, and at Mersa Matruh this resentment turned to an active if temporary dislike when the New Zealanders, partially encircled, fought their way out believing (incorrectly) that the 1st Armoured Division had left them in the lurch.

The entire climate changed when Montgomery arrived to command 8th Army. Incompetent commanders were sacked and the philosophy of dispersion was thrown to the winds, being replaced by an orthodoxy the like of which had not been seen in the desert since O'Connor's day. The

Desert workshops; in the left background a Sherman dwarfs a Valentine, with a Crusader, more Valentines and a Stuart nearer the camera. On the right is a rare Covenanter.

keynote of this was concentration. The armour would fight *en masse* with concentrated artillery support, and battle drills would be strictly adhered to. Unlike Rommel, who was prepared to gamble, Montgomery intended to invest only in certainties.

More British armour fought at Second Alamein than in any other battle in North Africa. For the armoured divisions this was not a battle of wide, sweeping movements across the desert, but a dog-fight which reached its climax at Tel el Aqqaqir on 2 November 1942 as part of the operation known as 'Supercharge'. This had begun the previous night when two infantry brigades from 50th and 51st Divisions—operating under the control of 2nd New Zealand Division—had with their Infantry tanks blown a corridor through the Axis minebelt and forward infantry defences. Through this at dawn passed the 9th Armoured Brigade on a mission that was little short of a death ride—to wipe out the enemy's anti-tank gun screen and, if necessary, incur 100 per cent casualties in doing so. The task was accomplished at a cost of 75 out of 94 tanks and, as intended, succeeded in drawing Panzerarmee Afrika onto the battlefield, to be met in turn by the 1st Armoured Division pouring through the broken line. In the day-long battle which followed the British lost slightly more tanks, but Rommel's armour was virtually written off.

In the pursuit which followed the armoured divisions reaped the harvest of victory, but were initially hindered by bad going caused by heavy rain. During the advance across Africa to the Tunisian frontier only comparatively minor actions were fought.

The Tank Brigades

The tank brigades were trained and equipped specifically to support infantry operations and were for the first years of the war known as Army Tank Brigades, although one formation, the 23rd Armoured Brigade, retained its original title throughout. Three Infantry tank regiments constituted a tank brigade, although they rarely fought together as a formation and the function of brigade headquarters was largely administrative.

In general, a regiment supported an infantry brigade, a squadron a battalion, and a troop a company. Operational control rested with the infantry commander unless enemy armour sought to intervene, when the tanks fought as squadrons and regiments under the control of their own officers.

The Infantry tank regiment was organised similarly to the armoured regiment, with minor variations. Close Support Matildas served in the squadron headquarters of Matilda regiments and the first Valentine regiments to reach North Africa. No CS version of the Valentine was produced, however, and as the stocks of CS Matildas dwindled this left Valentine regiments entirely without the ability to engage with high explosive. At Second Alamein this was remedied by up-grading the all-Valentine 23rd Armoured Brigade to brigade group status by adding a regiment of Bishop self-propelled guns which were on immediate call.

Teamwork between tanks, infantry and artillery was the essence of the set-piece attack. As originally practised, the battle drill began with an artillery bombardment of the objective. While this was still falling, the first wave of tanks would break into the position and subdue the immediate opposition. The second wave would arrive some minutes later, the timing being such that the enemy should not be able to put to good use any recovery he might have made after the initial shock of being overrun. The infantry would arrive just behind the second wave and should be faced only with disorganised and demoralised survivors. The tanks would then remain with the infantry until their anti-tank guns were brought up and the position consolidated against counter-attack. On being released by the infantry commander, the tanks would withdraw a little distance to a Forward Rally where they would repair minor damage and replenish fuel and ammunition. The Forward Rally was regarded as the point where the next attack would be won and was organised to operate at top speed so that the tanks could report themselves available to the infantry commander who was to continue the advance.

This type of attack was carried out in daylight throughout the desert war and in Tunisia, with the exception of Second Alamein where the infantry

1. Light tank Mk VIB, 'C'Sqn., 1 RTR, 7th Armd.Div.; May 1940

2. Light tank Mk VIB, 'C'Sqn., 1 RTR, August 1940

1. A9 of Brig.A.C.Willison, HQ 32 Army Tk. Bde.; November 1941

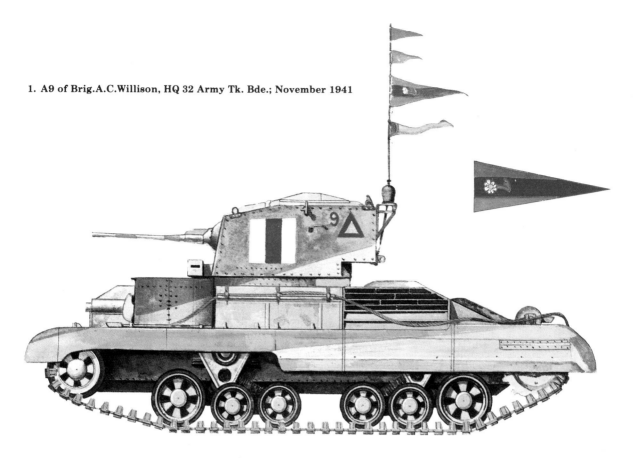

2. A10, 2 RTR, 7th Armd. Bde., 7th Armd.Div.; May 1941

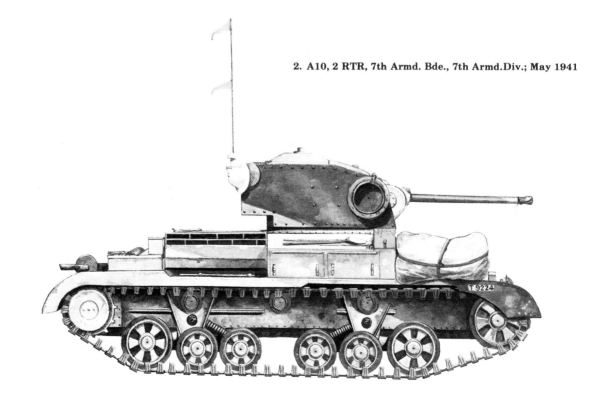

B

1. A13, Advance HQ, 2nd Armd.Div.; February 1941

2. Crusader I, 'C'Sqn., 10th Hussars, 2nd Armd.Bde.,
1st Armd.Div.; February 1942

3. Crusader II, 'A' Sqn., 9th Lancers, 2nd Armd.Bde.,
1st Armd.Div.; Alamein, October 1942

C

Gamecock II

GRIMSBY

DUCK

T10064

DONOVAN

T6837 DRAKE

1. Matilda, 'A'Sqn., 4 RTR, 32 Army Tk. Bde., November 1941

2. Matilda, 42 RTR, 1 Army Tk.Bde.; 25 November 1941

D

1. Valentine II, 'C'Sqn., 40 RTR, 23rd Armd. Bde.,
8th Armd.Div.; 22 July 1942

2. Valentine II, 'C'Sqn., 40 RTR; September 1942

1. Stuart I of Brig.A.Gatehouse, 4th Light Armd.Bde., 7th Armd.Div.; November 1941

2. Aerial pennants and signal flags; see Plates commen for detailed explanations.

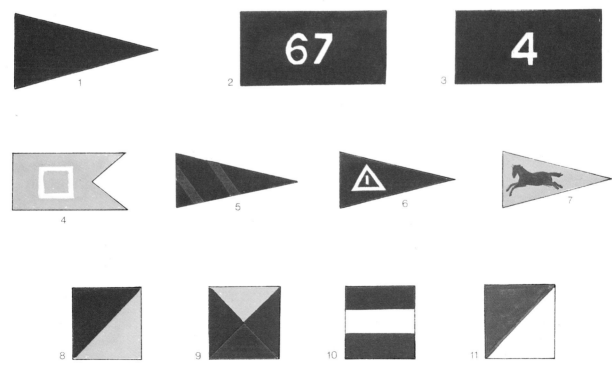

F

1. Grant I, 'C'Sqn., 3 RTR, 7th Armd. Div.; May 1942

2. Gen.Montgomery's 'charger', 8th Army Tac HQ;
   October 1942 - January 1943

1. Sherman II, 'C'Sqn., 3rd Hussars, 9th Armd.Bde.;
Alamein, 2 November 1942

2. Sherman III, Royal Scots Greys; December 1942

H

attacked mainly at night; and here another drill, carefully rehearsed prior to the war, was carried out. The infantry led and the tanks followed closely behind with the object of being in very close support at first light. Having seized the objective, the infantry were very vulnerable to counter-attack until their own anti-tank guns could be brought up to form a defensive screen, and until they did arrive the tanks took over this rôle as well as providing direct fire support. Sometimes, if the distance to the objective was considerable, the infantry would ride on the tanks to a pre-determined startline and would then proceed ahead on foot. The technique worked extremely well and Rommel later recorded his professional interest in it, commenting that 'the British storming parties would work their way up to our positions, accompanied by tanks which acted as mobile artillery, and would force their way into the trenches at the point of the bayonet. Everything went methodically and according to a drill.'

Within the framework described above there were numerous minor tactical situations which arose as a result of local checks. During these each arm dealt with problems which were causing the other difficulties; for example the tanks knocked out machine gun posts which pinned down the infantry, and the latter stalked anti-tank guns which held up the armour; through its Forward Observation Officers, who usually rode with the tanks, the artillery applied fire support as and where it was required.

Prior to the autumn of 1940 no Infantry tank unit was present in North Africa and the arrival of 7 RTR, equipped with Matildas, was concealed from the Italians until Operation 'Compass'. Within 24 hours the regiment, supporting 4th Indian Division, stormed its way through the fortified camps at Nibeiwa and Tummar and then ran riot inside Sidi Barrani itself. In January 1941, fighting with 6th Australian Division, it broke the back of resistance at Bardia and then at Tobruk.

A second Matilda regiment, 4 RTR, arrived in the spring of 1941 and, as already described, was brigaded with 7 RTR for the ill-fated Operation 'Battleaxe'. What could have been a disaster was avoided when one squadron from each regiment respectively held off both Panzer divisions for several hours until the British withdrawal had been completed.

During 'Crusader' no less than five 'I' tank regiments were involved in the relief of Tobruk. Inside the fortress was 32nd Army Tank Brigade, incorporating 1 RTR (actually armed with Cruisers), 4 RTR and 'D' Sqn. 7 RTR. ('A' and 'B' squadrons 7 RTR were at this time employed on tank delivery—by tradition, the regiment lettered its third squadron 'D'.) Supporting the infantry of 13 Corps in their drive on the right flank of the relief operation were the three regiments of 1st Army Tank Brigade, 8 RTR with Valentines, and 42 and 44 RTR with Matildas.

13 Corps by-passed Halfaya Pass, Sollum and Bardia, but was forced to storm the fortified zones of Omar Nuovo, Libyan Omar and Fort Capuzzo which lay astride its lines of communication. The Omars were captured by 4th Indian Division and the two Matilda regiments, in spite of the presence of '88's at both locations, and Capuzzo was taken by 2nd New Zealand Division with 8 RTR in support. Meanwhile the Tobruk garrison had launched a breakout operation, led by 70th Division and 32nd Army Tank Brigade, and had progressed as far as Ed Duda. By 25 November 13 Corps had reached Belhamed, a mile or two away. The two forces joined hands the next day, following a brilliantly planned night attack led by 44 RTR. The Corps' operations had been conducted with a smooth efficiency throughout, aided by the fact that Rommel allowed himself to become completely absorbed in the great tank battle with 7th Armoured Division to the south, and then embarked on his fruitless Dash to the Wire. On 31 December 1941 Bardia was stormed for the second time, the attack of 2nd South African Division being led by 8 and 44 RTR, and Sollum was captured soon after. The Axis garrison of Halfaya Pass, completely isolated, held out until 17 January.

During the Gazala/Knightsbridge fighting the tank brigades fared as unhappily as the rest of the British armour. When Rommel attacked, both were lying just behind the line of infantry boxes which stretched from Gazala to Bir Hacheim: in the north was 32nd Army Tank Brigade, with 7 RTR and two squadrons of 42

Stuart I 'Cresta Run'—a name perpetuated by 8th King's Royal Irish Hussars on its tanks in NW Europe. The crewman, in the hot, unpopular, and soon-discarded US tank helmet, holds the 'Action' flag—see Plate F2/9.

RTR; further south was 1st Army Tank Brigade, with 44 RTR and one squadron of 42 RTR. 8 RTR had been detached for specific operations and 4 RTR, recently converted to Valentines, did not arrive until the battle had begun.

When the Afrika Korps swept round the southern end of the line on 27 May, 44 RTR launched an attack into the flank of 21. Panzer-Division, obliterating a motor rifle regiment but losing 18 Matildas in the process. The remainder of the regiment's tanks withdrew into the 150th Brigade Box and were fought to destruction when this was stormed.

On 5 June the long delayed and unco-ordinated British assault on the Cauldron took place. On the northern flank the 70 Matildas of 32nd Army Tank Brigade were to attack Sidra Ridge, accompanied by a Valentine squadron of 8 RTR. In theory this hammer blow should have smashed in the Axis flank, but actually resulted in such a stunning failure that the action became known as the Sidra Puzzle. First, the tanks rolled over an unmarked minefield; those which emerged were engaged by '88's firing invisibly from the east with the rising sun behind them, the glare preventing the British crews from making effective reply. 7 and 42 RTR suffered such severe losses that they were forced to combine their remaining resources. On 13 June Rommel attempted to

isolate the 201st Guards Brigade Box at Knightsbridge by a pincer movement. One thrust was met and held by 7/42 RTR in a day-long action, and the other was contained by 8 RTR.

The battle was, however, irretrievably lost by now, and a general withdrawal to Egypt began while preparations were made for Tobruk to stand a second siege. The garrison included 32nd Army Tank Brigade, consisting of 4 and 7 RTR, both with Valentines, although the 7th retained a few Matildas and five Grants taken over from 1 RTR; both fought to the last tank when the fortress fell on 20 June.

The tank brigades' season of disaster had yet another month to run. On 22 July two regiments (40 and 46 RTR) of the recently arrived all-Valentine 23rd Armoured Brigade were committed to an attack which it was hoped would break the German line at Ruweisat Ridge. 23rd and 24th Armoured Brigades belonged originally to the 8th Armoured Division, which had trained with Valentines in the United Kingdom and was shipped with them to Egypt. The division never fought as a formation. None of the stated pre-conditions for the attack existed, but it was ordered just the same in the cynical belief that the new arrivals would not only be unaffected by the general tiredness and despondency, but would also be unaware of the inherent dangers and carry out the advance without hesitation. They did, some of their vehicles even breaking through to engage the DAK headquarters' own anti-tank guns before being picked off; this was achieved at a cost of 93 out of 104 tanks shot to pieces on an anti-tank gun killing ground.

Together, Sidra and Ruweisat led to opinions being expressed by the less thoughtful that the 'I' tank had had its day. The more perceptive realised that both actions represented a departure from orthodox principles in attempting to use the slow, under-gunned vehicles in the armoured brigade rôle. It was Montgomery who restored the balance, recognising that the forthcoming battle would be entirely positional and that the need for Infantry tanks had actually increased.

Of 8th Army's original Infantry tank regiments, 4 and 7 RTR had been lost at Tobruk and 42 and 44 RTR had been so badly mauled in the Gazala battle that they could only provide crews to man the Scorpion flail detachments. Only 8 RTR remained battleworthy, and was posted to 23rd Armoured Brigade, which became the army's specialist Infantry tank formation.

During Second Alamein the brigade (8, 40, 46, and 50 RTR) supported troops from 1st South African, 2nd New Zealand, 4th Indian, 9th Australian, 50th Northumbrian and 51st Highland Divisions, their combined function being to 'open the door' for the armoured divisions to pass through. Its regiments earned unstinting praise from whoever they worked with, none more than 40 RTR, who stood off 21. Panzer-Division's counter-attack on 9th Australian Division at Thompson's Post, trading four vehicles for every one of the enemy's knocked out but refusing to budge an inch.

For most of the advance to Tripoli the brigade was reduced to a single regiment, 40 RTR, which operated under the command of 51st Highland Division. Because its tanks snapped so often around the heels of the 90th Light's rear-guards the Jocks christened the regiment 'Monty's Foxhounds', a title which stuck and which received the approval of the Army Commander; it was, in fact, the only unit ever to bear his name. Infantry tank brigades were prominent and notably successful in the later Tunisian fighting, of which some relevant account is given in Vanguard No. 13, *The Churchill Tank*.

The hard, grinding rôle of the Tank Brigades was less vulnerable to unorthodoxy than that of the armoured divisions and, because of this, their success was generally more consistent. It was a vital rôle, too often ignored, and without it the campaign would have taken a very different course. The hard-won Victoria Cross was awarded only twice to RTR personnel during the Second World War, on both occasions to Infantry tank officers serving in the desert: one recipient was Capt. Phillip Gardner of 4 RTR for an action which took place during the Tobruk garrison's break-out in November 1941, and the second was Lt.Col. H. R. B. Foote of 7 RTR for actions performed during the Gazala battle.

Grant crew of 2nd Royal Gloucestershire Hussars, 22nd Armd.Bde., pose in front of their apparently unmarked tank.

Vehicle Recovery and Delivery

Without a reliable vehicle recovery, repair and delivery organisation no mechanised army can survive long in the field. In this respect the British were rather more efficient than the Axis, although high vehicle losses naturally resulted from defeats such as 'Battleaxe', when the enemy was left in possession of the battlefield. In simplified terms, the essential workings of the organisation—the responsibility of the Royal Army Ordnance Corps until the formation of the Royal Electrical and Mechanical Engineers—paralleled RAMC casualty clearance procedure in which wounded men were passed back through the Regimental Aid Post, Advanced Dressing Station, Forward Surgical Unit and on to a Base Hospital, with each stage absorbing a higher level of injury.

In vehicular terms, the first stage was the armoured regiment's own Light Aid Detachment. If the damage was beyond the LAD's capacity the regiment's technical adjutant would radio details to the brigade recovery officer, using a lettered code. This included such information as L—left hand; M—mined; N—clutch burned out; P—engine seized; Q—belly blown in, and so on. Thus an encoded message 'T12345 G678910 MQSRTU' would be understood by the Brigade Recovery Section as 'Tank No. 12345, at grid reference 678910, with mine damage to its belly, suspension damage, right hand track blown off, and unserviceable transmission'. The Recovery Section was then despatched, along with a detachment from Brigade Workshops which would assist in on-site repairs to tracks, suspension, engine etc., until the tank could be towed or driven to ground accessible to tank transporters and then back-loaded to the Workshops. Unless the suspension was intact enough for towing, burned-out tanks were abandoned, although repairable turrets would be salvaged, and suspensions from 'brew-ups' would be cannibalised to get other tanks moving.

Repairs beyond Brigade Workshops' capacity, e.g. penetrations of and damage to transmissions, were back-loaded to a 3rd Echelon unit, the Tank Troops Workshops; if TTW were unable to cope, the tank would generally be back-loaded by rail to Base Workshops.

March 1942: Grant 'T-24700' of 'C' Sqn., 3 RTR is prepared for action. The old 'His Majesty's Tank' formula has been re-adopted—see name above WD number. The new signals procedure is evident from the '10B' marked inside the squadron circle; see also Plate G1. This tank was lost, along with T-24725, T-23544 and T-24243 near Bir Harmat on 30 May during the Gazala Line battles.

At all levels in the chain, suitable areas where transporters had hard ground and manoeuvring space for picking up derelicts were chosen and designated Collecting Points. Most recovery operations took place by night, as did most back-loading, to fit in with Corps movement control timetables. When things were going badly the tempo of back-loading had to be accelerated sharply.

At the start of 'Knightsbridge' Col. P. W. H. Whiteley was appointed Army Recovery Officer, and was immediately forced to think several stages ahead of normal procedure. 'The buggering about between Bir Hacheim and Capuzzo and Tobruk and Sidi Rezegh had to be seen to be believed. My orders were to beat the Germans at the recovery game. I was given a first-class radio network and we linked this in to divisions, and listened on regimental frequencies to "guesstimate" where to apply our back-up and scarce resources.'

As the battle swung Rommel's way the LADs and Bde. Workshops performed prodigies which have never been sufficiently recognised. Whiteley's problem was handling 3rd and 4th Line casualties,

and this was tackled in two ways. First, the 'badly wounded' tanks were taken to the Capuzzo or Fuka rail-heads, and shipped on flat-cars back to the base area production line facilities. Secondly, 'dead and dying' tanks were concentrated as far forward as possible, with the *minimum* of back-loading. Well apart from the Collecting Points, these tank graveyards were termed 'Help Yourself Dumps'; and apart from providing cannibalisation facilities, they caused the enemy to waste precious shells on what he imagined were AFV leaguers. During the retreat to Alamein crippled vehicles were blown up by recovery teams in danger of being overrun; Whiteley's own group demolished a Grant so effectively that it blocked three priceless railway tracks at Fuka, and after Second Alamein he was interested to observe that his Axis opposite numbers had been unable to remove it. The overall success of Whiteley's efforts can be judged by the fact that a good percentage of the tanks which fought at Alamein had been recovered during 'Knightsbridge' and the retreat.

Surprisingly, it was only after discussions between Whiteley and the commander of the RASC tank transporter column that a logical working relationship was established between the two organisations, which solved problems for both.

Transporters saved track-mileage by bringing regiments forward from rail-heads to operational areas; they also carried new and repaired tanks up to armoured formations' Forward Delivery Sqns. (see below), but would then return to rail-head empty. The empty trailers suffered numerous weld failures due to vibration sufficient 'to wake Beethoven' (who, it will be recalled, was not merely dead, but deaf as well); there was seldom time for the tiresome chore of ballasting them. Whiteley's liaison led to an agreement whereby transporters would proceed to Collecting Points after making their forward deliveries, where the expert Recovery crews would load their cripples for back-loading to the rail-head. A consequent benefit was the immediate drop in the incidence of trailer failures.

Forward Delivery Sqns. were another essential link in the chain, and performed two functions for their respective armoured formations. They held the unwounded crews of knocked-out tanks,

Grants of RHQ, 'B' and 'C' Sqns., 5 RTR, perform for the camera in February 1942. They are in overall Light Stone and unmarked; but the nearest has a squadron commander's pennant in red over light blue—battalion colours. The Stuart is probably an RHQ tank, flying navigator's multiple pennants.

as well as replacement crews, until they could be found vehicles; and they delivered new and repaired tanks to regiments by means of those crews. At first their organisation was rather sketchy; as mentioned elsewhere, during 'Crusader' the Army's two forward delivery squadrons were in fact 'A' and 'B' Sqns., 7 RTR.

Finally, it is worth mentioning what was almost certainly the longest 'lift' of the entire campaign, when 50 RTR were sent up to rejoin 23rd Armd.Bde. during the advance on Tripoli. The tanks were loaded on to transporters near Alamein at the end of November 1942, and were not unloaded until 8 January 1943, ten miles west of Nofilia in Tripolitania—a run of 1,000 miles.

The Plates

(Research and captions by David List)

A1: Light Tank Mk VIB, 'C' Sqn., 1 RTR, 7th Armoured Division; May 1940

Shipped to Egypt in 1938 in overall sand colour with random orange patterning, 1 RTR's tanks were overall sand by the outbreak of war; they carried the Mobile Division Egypt formation sign and the divisional unit serial number in white on red on right and left front dustguards respectively, as viewed. The jerboa was added to complete the now-famous formation sign after May 1940. Squadron tactical markings were of the solid colours specified for tank battalions, in red for 'A', yellow for 'B' and blue for 'C'; battalion HQ marked in battalion colour, i.e. red. Black bridge signs on yellow were carried on the nose, and tank WD numbers in white or black on each hull side, although these were often obliterated during painting. Tanks of 1 RTR were named with the initial letter 'A', following First World War tradition, in white on the battalion's red.

A2: Light Tank Mk VIB, 'C' Sqn., 1 RTR; August 1940

May 1940 saw several experiments in camouflage by 7th Armoured Div. which culminated in the 'Caunter Scheme' devised by Brig. Caunter, CO of the old Heavy Armoured Bde. which became 4th Armoured Bde.; this was in slanted horizontal areas of Black, Green and Light Stone, from top to bottom. WD numbers were overpainted, and often bridge signs also. By August the jerboa had been added to some but not all tanks. The old

5 RTR Grant crewman in second pattern US tank helmet, giving the 'Rally' signal with semaphore flags.

civilian registration plates were sandblasted clean —see rear view—but in 'Aberdeen's' case it has been retouched in black. Squadron signs were unchanged. (Cavalry units seem to have favoured an outlined style, with white troops numbers alongside—the patch view shows that of a tank of 8th Hussars, whose unit serial number was '25'.) Pennants followed troop colouring for troop leaders and were plain red on other tanks, and were flown in the 'position of the day' to indicate friendly forces—here, 'two top'. Aerial bases were sometimes white for night recognition, sometimes natural black.

B1: Cruiser Mk I (A9), Brig. A. C. Willison, HQ 32 Army Tank Bde.; Operation 'Crusader', November 1941

Following rough handling in the first German offensive of March 1941, 3rd Armoured Bde. was withdrawn into the Tobruk perimeter where, in October, it was renamed 32 Army Tank Bde., under the command of Brig. A. C. Willison. The brigade was built up into a potent force in the months before 'Crusader'; and two old A9s dug in on Derna Road airfield after mechanical breakdown during the March operations were recovered by the Brigade Light Repair Section and refitted by the Workshops as command tanks. Willison's tank is finished in Slate and Silver-Grey over Light Stone, and seems to have retained its old markings without additional insignia: the 'A' Sqn. triangle and the number '9' on the turret. Ahead of this is seen the white and red recognition flash ordered for this operation on both turret sides and the front dustguards. Blue pennants were flown in the 'position of the day' for 17–26 November ('two top'); and below them is the brigade command pennant in brown, red and green with the brigade's marguerite flower insignia in white, yellow and green. Note that a woman's stocking is also flown from the base of the aerial!

B2: Cruiser Mk IIA (A10), 2 RTR, 7th Armoured Bde., 7th Armoured Div.; Operation 'Brevity', May 1941

Detached from 3rd Armoured Bde. in the UK and sent to reinforce 7th Armoured Div. in time for Operation 'Compass' in December 1940, 2 RTR

landed in UK camouflage with their full range of markings. They were overpainted in 'light sandy coloured paint with black-grey camouflage patterns'. T.9224 was a replacement tank collected on 16 April 1941 and later handed over by 2 RTR to 7th Hussars on 9 July 1941. No attempt has been made to add markings. The tank seems to have been finished in Light Stone with Purple-Brown and Silver-Grey overstriping. The WD number has been repainted in black and the aerial mounting in white. Yellow pennants, one top, one middle, were ordered for 14 May.

C1: Cruiser Mk IVA (A13 Mk II), Advance HQ, 2nd Armoured Div.; February 1941

The division arrived in the Middle East in December 1940 with the 1st and 3rd Armoured Brigades. Advance HQ was formed in January 1941 with five ACVs, two 'chargers' (one for the GOC and one for his ADC), three Cruisers and three Light tanks for the Protection Troop, and eleven Scout Cars. Before ever seeing action the Cruisers were transferred to the 7th Armoured Div., and 1st Armoured Bde. was sent to Greece. When the depleted division was sent into action it was caught and smashed by Rommel's first offensive, two of the ACVs being appropriated by Rommel and Streich for their own use. This A13

Mk II of the HQ Squadron carries the divisional formation sign, a white knight's helm on red, on the left of the turret rear plate, and the divisional unit serial number '40' in white on black on the right. The personal name 'Evelyn' and the WD number (unconfirmed) are both in white. The tank is finished in overall Light Stone with overstriping of Slate and Silver-Grey.

C2: Cruiser Mk VI, Crusader I (A15), 'C' Sqn., 10th Hussars, 2nd Armoured Bde., 1st Armoured Div.; February 1942

The Crusaders of the 10th Hussars were painted overall Light Stone without overstriping. The divisional unit serial number was carried in white on red on the left front dustguard, as viewed, and the division's formation sign, a white rhino on a black oval, on the right; they were repeated in reverse order on the rear of the tank. Squadron tactical markings and names were in blue throughout the regiment, and pennants were

Orders Group round a Sherman III of HQ. 24th Armd.Bde., masquerading under its 'truck' disguise.

normally in the same colour; the example illustrated is the recognition sign for 2nd Armoured Bde. in the period before Operation 'Lightfoot'. The WD number T.15750 is in black.

C3: Cruiser Mk VI, Crusader II (A15), 9th Lancers, 2nd Armoured Bde., 1st Armoured Div.; Operation 'Lightfoot', October 1942

Unlike the Shermans of the rest of the regiment, which were camouflaged by an RE Camouflage Unit, the Crusaders grouped together in 'A' Sqn. and RHQ seem generally to have retained their old Light Stone overall finish; some at least had wavy white lines painted at random over the hull sides, indicating the borders of the new camouflage scheme which was about to be applied when the Camouflage Unit was called away, leaving them unfinished. The tank name is in black, flanked by the divisional unit serial number in white on red, and by an obliterated formation sign suggesting that this is a replacement tank. The 'A' Sqn. marking is painted in yellow on the right turret side, as viewed. One red and one white pennant are flown centrally, the sequence for 26 October 1942. The black signboard with a chalked '401' indicates the tank's place in the column for the passage of the minefield gap. We illustrate a possible regimental pennant in red and black, indicating either a squadron leader or a navigator's tank.

D1: Infantry Tank Mk II, Matilda (A12), 'A' Sqn., 4 RTR, 32 Army Tank Bde.; Operation 'Crusader', November 1941

Regular battalions of the RTR maintained a tradition of naming their tanks with the initial letter which corresponded to their own number. When 4 RTR arrived in the desert in 1941 the majority of their 'D-names' were painted on the hull sides, although in some cases the name also appears on the front plate as well. 7 RTR painted their 'G-names' on the sides of the driving compartment, although an unusual style seen during 'Battleaxe' was 'Gamecock II' commanded by Maj. J. Holden, OC 'A' Sqn., and driven by Cpl. Les Bowie, a former film special-effects man—hence the artistic licence! We also illustrate the normal lettering, e.g. 'Grimsby'. At Nibeiwa one 7 RTR Matilda carried a skull centrally on the nose; the WD number is unfortunately unknown. 'Duck' and 'Donovan' show typical slight variations in the style of marking names on front and rear plates of 4 RTR Matildas.

All the Army Tank Bde. battalions retained individually coloured squadron insignia enclosing the troop number, in white for the squadron leader and in squadron colour for other tanks. For the defence of Tobruk and the break-out to join up with 13 Corps white numbers were painted on the hull sides of 4 RTR and 'D' Sqn. 7 RTR squadron leaders' tanks. For 'Crusader' 4 RTR flew blue recognition pennants, with command pennants below them where appropriate. A tin sheet 'pennant' in blue with a white '1' is fixed ahead of the cupola on 'Drake'. White and red recognition flashes were ordered specifically for 'Crusader' because the enemy were known to be using some captured British tanks; they proved highly unpopular as they offered the enemy an excellent aiming point, and were scrubbed over with sand and oil soon after the link-up had been achieved.

D2: Infantry Tank Mk II, Matilda (A12), 42 RTR, 1 Army Tank Bde.; Operation 'Crusader', 25 November 1941

While attacking successfully at Omar Nuovo and Libyan Omar with two squadrons of 42 and one of 44 RTR, 1st Army Tank Bde. lost heavily to the

German anti-tank guns; their 'crocks' were collected at the brigade's Light Recovery Section in the Sidi Azeiz area. On the morning of the 25th 16 Matildas were concentrated there, some on their tracks and some on Scammell transporters, with ammunition and stowage removed and piled alongside in readiness for repair work on the tanks. It was then that a German Panzer group caught them by chance, and advanced for a quick 'kill'. The dismounted crews of 42 RTR at once manned their 'dead' tanks, and managed to fight off the enemy long enough for the technical personnel and stores trucks to escape. On their return some hours later they found all the Matildas and several Panzers wrecked and smoking, and the British crews dead around their 'lame ducks'.

Both 42 and 44 RTR were Territorial battalions, and named their tanks from the initials of the alphabet 'second time around', giving 42 'P-names' and 44 'R-names'. ('Phantom', T.6968, was the CO's tank of 42 RTR in the battle for the Omars.) The brigade's red diabolo sign and unit serials were carried by some but not all tanks—'Phantom' did display it, and we have shown it on this tank. Many had the slanted horizontal straight-edged camouflage pattern, and the AFV identity flashes for 'Crusader'. We have illustrated this example in a scheme of Light Stone with Green and Purple-Brown overstriping.

E1: Infantry Tank Mk III, Valentine II, 'C' Sqn., 40 RTR, 23rd Armoured Bde., 8th Armoured Div.; Operation 'Splendour', 22 July 1942

23rd Armoured Bde. was shipped to the Middle

Grainy but classic study of the cast-hull M4A1 Sherman IIs of The Queen's Bays at Second Alamein. Camouflage is Green over Desert Pink, and although the censor has been at work, the fronts of the dustguards bear (left as viewed) the rhino sign of 1st Armd.Div. and (right) the unit serial '85' in white on red—a reversal of the usual positions. T.145063 is nearest the camera; names are not visible in photos of these tanks, but the regiment usually called its vehicles after racehorses. Note .50 cal. turret guns. (RAC Tank Museum)

East pre-painted and partially ready for battle, although much remained to be done in the way of tropicalising their radios and acclimatising the crews. Tanks from both 23rd and 24th Armoured Bdes. were assembled to bring 23rd up to strength. 2/Lt. E. L. Wiard, commanding 10 Tp., 'C' Sqn., was mounted in his own 'Culloden', however. Note that the 'Go' sign of 8th Armoured Div. was still displayed. The Middle East scheme had been applied over the temperate pattern camouflage,

Beneath the censor's marks the original contact print of this shot reveals the 1st Armd.Div. rhino above the unit serial '71' on the nearest trackguard—identifying a Sherman II of HQ, 2nd Armd.Bde. The Desert Pink finish of T.145029 has been marked with a white guideline by a Camouflage Unit, who were called away before completing the painting of the Brigade's tanks, leaving some of them to fight at Second Alamein like this. The far tank is named 'Antick'. (The white lines suggest a probable origin for other well-known colour-schemes of the period involving apparent white trim around the darker of two or more camouflage colours—this is noticeable on Priests and Grants.)

with traces showing through, and an area of green exposed in the squadron/troop mark on the turret. No pennants were flown on 22 July. This gallant officer actually reached the brigade's final objective under a hail of fire from the DAK's HQ screen of anti-tank guns before being knocked out and made prisoner. The blue pennant, 6ins. × 9ins., was flown on the tank of the brigadier at this date; for details of other command pennants see F2.

E2: Infantry Tank Mk III, Valentine II, 'C' Sqn., 40 RTR, 23rd Armoured Bde.; September 1942

After the disaster of 'Splendour' 40 RTR were quickly brought up to strength to save the battalion from being disbanded—the fate of 24th Armoured Bde. after Operations 'Lightfoot' and 'Supercharge'. There was little time and less inclination to maintain a full set of markings, with

the regiment continuously in the forward area either in action or on 'schemes' in preparation for 'Lightfoot'. This is probably a replacement tank completed in Light Stone and Green by Ordnance. The only marking is the name 'Cheetah' carefully painted in red shadowed with black on the nose plate; it was repeated in slightly smaller characters centrally on the hull rear plate. Two red pennants are flown, as a recognition mark; and as the tank is fitted with a sun compass the other is probably the blue flag indicating a navigator's vehicle, a known alternative to the long, square-ended black streamer which often identified a navigator.

For Operation 'Lightfoot' 46 RTR of this brigade were issued with twelve 'Anti-Mine Roller Attachments' or 'Fowler Rollers'. Five Valentines so fitted joined the unit on its march to the start line and then led the tanks into battle on 23 October. They were used again on the 28th, and proved a useful addition to the RE gapping teams and Scorpions, who suffered heavy casualties both from mines and from aimed fire. By the time the minefields were breached all five Valentines were out of action, taking no further part in the Alamein operations. Photos indicate a general

Matilda Scorpions were first used to gap minefields during Operation 'Lightfoot', and performed well, although all 12 became casualties. Note station-keeping lights on rods behind turret.

colour scheme very similar to 'Cheetah', completely without insignia.

F1: Light Tank M3, Stuart I, Brig. A. Gatehouse, HQ Sqn., 4th Armoured Bde., 7th Armoured Div.; Operation 'Crusader', November 1941

For 'Crusader' the whole brigade was equipped with 'Honeys'; and although outranged and under-armed in comparison with the German tanks they gave a good account of themselves by the use of flexible tactics and superior speed, under the calm direction of Brig. Gatehouse. The brigadier exercised this control from a comfortable deck chair on the rear deck of his own 'charger', which we illustrate here.

Gatehouse was luckily absent when the night leaguer of the Brigade HQ and the 8th Hussars was overrun by a German battle-group. He later rose to command 10th Armoured Div. at Alamein. His M3 is unremarkable; it is finished in Light Stone and Silver-Grey, with white-red-

Wolves in sheep's clothing, and sheep in wolves' clothing . . . Dummy tank units to misdirect enemy Intelligence were created in 'gaps' in the RTR numbering sequence; '30', '60' and '100' series RTR battalions appeared and disappeared at the behest of 'A' Force and its commander, the remarkable Brig. Dudley Clarke. During Operation 'Crusader' two such units, 10 RTR and 'F' RTR, successfully threatened the German flank from concentrations around Siwa and Giarabub. In December 1941/January 1942 1st Army Tank Bde. had an extra Crusader regiment, 101 RTR; while 37 RTR ostensibly plugged the hole blown in 4th Armd.Bde. in November 1941 with 52 dummy M3s. (These units were manned by small detachments of tank and infantry troops—a dummy tank requires only a driver.) Dummies mingled with real units in the bitter May–August 1942 fighting, persuading the DAK that they *were* dummies. 'Sunshields' or truck disguises were continuously used to conceal tank strength until the moment of contact. Operation 'Bertram', the cover plan for 'Lightfoot', saw the fake 74th Armd.Bde.— 39, 118, and 124 RTR—moving into the positions vacated by the real armour when it moved up to battle positions for Second Alamein. The photos show: (below) mobile 'Crusaders', beautifully made of lath and canvas and flawlessly painted. These 101 RTR vehicles are built on trucks—note the exposed driver's position ahead of the fake turret. (top) The track-marking trailer towed behind them to fool air recce. (right) Truck disguises worn by an A13 and a Stuart.

white flashes on turret side and front dustguards, the HQ diamond in red on the turret, the divisional sign on the left front dustguard as viewed, and the WD number T.28174.

F2: Aerial pennants and signal flags
The use of aerial pennants fell into four main categories: (a) identification, friend or foe; (b) seniority within a unit or formation; (c) rank or position indicators; and (d) the passing of visual messages or orders.

Basic identification was by the number and position of small triangular pennants flown on a particular day or for a particular operation, as instructed by higher formation orders. Colour was not distinguishable at any distance, so position was the main identification; many of the colour plate captions give specific examples of these—e.g. 'two top', a popular formula, since it allowed ID at the greatest possible distance. Since units in the desert were far from sources of supply, replacement pennants were often improvised, more or less carefully. (As a general comment on

the whole use of pennants, one should bear in mind not only the impossibility of operating a complex system under combat conditions, but also the British Army's cherished tradition of 'tribal peculiarities'.)

The colour of the ID pennants was normally determined by seniority of a squadron within a regiment or a regiment within a brigade, based on the sequence red, yellow, blue; if necessary to accommodate more units, green and white were supposed to be used by fourth and fifth senior units. Thus the senior (oldest) regiment in a brigade flew red pennants, and so forth. Since

units were transferred fairly frequently, however, and since a replacement unit might be of greater or lesser seniority than the original unit according to which 17th-, 18th- or 19th-century war had led to its original formation, these colours changed around within brigades at intervals. There is no point in trying to generalise from the particular, and no substitute for direct reference if trying to determine the colour flown by any given unit at any given date.

Rank and position flags and pennants varied considerably, but systems officially prescribed were obeyed in at least some cases. These flags were normally flown in addition to basic ID pennants. Variants in regimental or corps colours, with the addition of regimental or formation signs, were quite common.

Plate F2/1 is a brigade commander's pennant, 12ins. × 36ins., in the red adopted for the Light Bde. commander in early 1940; a similar pennant in green was flown by the Heavy Bde. commander, and the designs seem to have been retained when the designations were changed to 'senior' and 'junior' brigades within a division. See the typically free variation flown by Brig. Willison on Plate B1, however; and note that there was also some use of a 6in. × 9in. blue pennant by brigade commanders.

F2/2 is a battalion or regimental (depending on whether RTR or cavalry) commander's flag, 18ins × 36ins., in the colour of seniority within the brigade and bearing the unit serial number, as painted on the front and rear of the tanks. In this case it is the '67' on blue of 10th Hussars, 2nd Armd.Bde., 1st Armd.Div. in February 1942. A regimentally-coloured alternative is *F2/3*, that flown by Col. O'Carroll of 4 RTR for the Tobruk break-out battles. This is in the blue that has always been the distinctive colour of 4 RTR, and bears the actual battalion number. There are reports of flags in the RTR's brown, red and green stripes bearing actual battalion numbers; but a photo of this tank certainly appears to have a single-colour pennant.

F2/4 shows a regulation squadron commander's swallow-tailed pennant, 9ins. × 19ins., in regimental or squadron seniority colour (according to unit practice). It bears the squadron mark in white—here, the square of 'B' Sqn. on the yellow of either 'B' Sqn. or the second senior regiment in the brigade. Plain rectangles of colour, with or without squadron signs, were also common.

F2/5 demonstrates a troop commander's pennant, 9ins. × 13ins.; officially these were supposed to be made with a base of the squadron colour (red, yellow or blue), with two 2-in. bars of troop colour (red, yellow, blue, green, or white) applied diagonally. Thus the combination shown is for the leader of 9 Tp., the first troop of 'C' Sqn.—red bars on blue. When troop and squadron colour coincided it seems that the base was supposed to be black edged in squadron colour—e.g. 1 Tp. leader, 'A' Sqn. would fly a black pennant edged in red with two red bars. The maintenance of this wildly bureaucratic system under combat conditions must have been totally impossible in most cases.

Common alternatives were as *F2/6*—in squadron colour, bearing either a troop number or a combination of squadron mark and troop number: here, 1 Tp., 'A' Sqn. Less common was the sort of unit design shown as *F2/7*; it is believed that 3rd Hussars used squadron-colour pennants bearing the regiment's 'horse of Hanover' badge in troop colour—here, 8 Tp. commander in 'B' Sqn.

Flags used for passing orders or messages—normally hand-held on sticks, but in some cases they might be attached to aerials—remained basically the same throughout the campaign. *F2/8* is 'I am out of action'. From about April 1941 a plain red square was used for 'I am out of action in a minefield', after too many tanks had been lost going to investigate the original signal flown by a comrade. *F2/9* is the order flag for 'Action'; *F2/10*, 'Rally'; and *F2/11*, 'Come on'.

G1: Grant I, 'C' Sqn., 3 RTR, 4th Armoured Bde., 7th Armoured Div.; Gazala operations, May 1942
This unit, photographed in transit, had neatly painted tanks with highly professional insignia of cartoon characters—this example seems to be one of Walt Disney's 'Three Little Pigs' in fighting mood. The camouflage colours appear to be Light Stone, partially sprayed over the original Olive Drab, with blotches of Purple-Brown. Sadly, T-24243 was reduced to smoking junk at Bir Harmat on 30 May, along with three of its companions; but 15th and 21st Panzer had also

received a lacing.

G2: GOC's Grant, GHQ Troop, Protection Sqn., 8th Army Tac. HQ; Operations 'Lightfoot', 'Supercharge' and 'Fire-Eater', October 1942–January 1943
When Montgomery took over the 8th Army he decided not only to have a tactical HQ divorced from the bustle of Main HQ, but also to have an armoured element in this. The HQ was formed from elements of 6 RTR, who were re-forming after the Knightsbridge battles, plus armoured cars from British and South African units at different times, and a LAA Battery. GHQ Troop of the squadron consisted of the GOC's 'charger', a modified Grant, and a second for his Chief of Staff, both delivered on 13 October 1942. At the general's own suggestion his Grant was named 'Monty'. The crew were Maj. J. Poston (11th Hussars), ADC to the GOC; Lt.J. Mouldon, MC (6 RTR), radio operator; Sgt. 'Paddy' Kennedy (6 RTR), main gunner; Tpr. Fegan (6 RTR), loader; and Cpl. J. Fraser, BEM, MM (6 RTR), driver. The tank was finished in Green over Desert Pink; it bore the 8th Army sign on the front left dustguard, as viewed, and the name in black fancy lettering on white. Both the standard recognition pennants and the GOC's own personal flag in red/black/red were flown from the aerials. (A similar flag in red/white/red identified a Corps commander, and a red swallow-tail of this size a Divisional commander.)

H1: Sherman II (M4), 'C' Sqn., 3rd The King's Own Hussars, 9th Armoured Bde.; 'Meet of the Grafton Hounds'—Operation 'Supercharge', 2 November 1942
9th Armoured Bde. were employed as a steel bludgeon to smash in the Axis 'PAK-front' on the line designated 'Grafton'—this being a compliment to the MFH of the Grafton Hounds, who served with the Royal Wiltshire Yeomanry. One hundred per cent casualties were deemed acceptable to achieve the objective, and this was nearly the price the regiments of this all-cavalry brigade paid. Shermans were received very late by these units and there was little time to apply either camouflage schemes or regimental names; some carried the bare minimum of markings, as here—

the squadron tactical mark, the WD number, and the brigade formation sign and unit serial number. The RAF roundel was probably carried on the rear decking—see Vanguard 15, '*The Sherman Tank in British Service*', Plate A. Pennants were flown in the 'position of the day' in seniority colours—red for 3rd Hussars, yellow for the Royal Wiltshire Yeomanry, and blue for the Warwickshire Yeomanry. The white fernleaf on black of 2nd New Zealand Division was added after the operation, as a 'battle honour'.

The only Commonwealth tanks in the desert were the Australian and New Zealand divisional cavalry regiments, whose rôle was reconnaissance and flank protection. 6th Aust.Div.Cav. arrived in 1940 with carriers; on the fall of Bardia in January 1941 its 'A', 'B' and 'C' Sqns., known as 'Dingo', 'Rabbit' and 'Wombat' respectively, acquired Italian armour which they used for a short period, abandoning them as they broke down or ran dry. 'Dingo' had five M.11s and one M.13, and penetrated as far as the harbour during the Tobruk assault of 21 January; the other two squadrons each had two M.13s. In early 1941 the 7th and 9th Aust.Divs. arrived, the former minus its cavalry unit; and the 6th and 9th fought impressively in Vichy Syria with carriers, some Light tanks, and, briefly, captured R-35s. 6th and 7th Divs. left the Middle East early in 1942; 9th Div.Cav. was hastily re-equipped with Stuarts and Crusaders and brought from northern Syria to Egypt. This unit led the break-out in the coastal sector of the Alamein front on 3 November 1942, advancing more than 20 miles to ElDaba on that day.

The 2nd NZ Div.Cav. fought with carriers and Light tanks in Greece and during Operation 'Crusader'; re-equipped with Stuarts, they fought at Second Alamein with 9th Armd.Bde., and were prominent in the advance to Tunisia.

The photo shows the white 'roos painted prominently on the turrets and hulls of their Italian captures by 6th Australian Divisional Cavalry.

H2: Sherman III (M4A2), ex-41 RTR, 24th Armoured Bde., Operation 'Lightfoot', 23 October 1942; illustrated in use by Royal Scots Greys, 'HoneyHill', December 1942

Shermans of 24th Armoured Bde. retained the 'Go' sign of 8th Armoured Div., and used the unit serial sequence 71, 40, 86, 67. Large tank names were carried on the rear hull, and the RAF roundel on the engine deck. Squadron marks followed the usual colour sequence, but the 41st appear to have used large call-sign numbers on the turret in addition to these.

'Cocky' was knocked out in a minefield during Alamein; was recovered, repaired, passed on to 47 RTR, and then handed over to the Greys for Operation 'Fire-Eater'. The Greys seem to have obliterated the original formation sign, and to have added their own badge—halved white over black, with a green and purple thistle normally superimposed, but not evident on the photo from which we take this painting. 'Cocky' was finally knocked out again in the battle of 'Honey Hill' on 17 December 1942. Note the 'cancelled' call-sign in the 'C' Sqn. circle.

Notes sur les planches en couleur

A1: Le numéro blanc sur carré rouge indique le régiment dans la brigade; le rond blanc sur fond rouge indique la division—le jerboa fut ajouté quelques semaines plus tard. Cercle bleu = Escadron 'C'; tous les tanks de ce régiment avaient des noms commençant par 'A'. **A2:** Nouveau 'Caunter-camouflage'; et dessin définitif de l'emblème de division, avec jerboa. (Encart) Style de l'enseigne d'escadron et du numéro de peloton du 8ème Hussards, dont le numéro de série était '25'.

B1: Converti en tank de commandement, ce A9 a conservé ses identifications de l'escadron 'A', maintenant hors de service. Le général de brigade Willison a des fanions de reconnaissance aux couleurs de sa brigade et indiquant la position du jour, au dessus de son propre fanion aux couleurs du RTR avec rosette de la brigade—notez aussi le bas! **B2:** Pas d'identification; on reconnaît clairement le camouflage Caunter.

C1: L'enseigne de la division était un heaume de chevalier; '40' indique les quartiers généraux de la division; et 'Evelyn' le nom de ce tank. **C2:** Le rhinocéros, emblème de la division et le numéro de série du régiment étaient inversement répétés à l'arrière. Les signes distinctifs de l'escadron et les noms de ce regiment étaient peints en bleu. **C3:** Tank de remplacement, dont l'identification de division est effacée. '401' est sa position dans la colonne sur le point de franchir un passage dans un champ de mines.

D1: Tous les tanks 4RTR ont des noms commançant par 'D' et les 7RTR par 'G'. Les fanions bleus et les voyants rouges et blancs permettaient de reconnaître les tanks engagés dans l'Opération 'Crusader'. **D2:** Un héros du combat—voué à l'échec—par des tanks endommagés à Sidi Azeiz le 25 novembre 1941; les noms des tanks du 42RTR commençaient par 'P' et certains portaient le signe de la brigade et le numéro de série du régiment, ici 173.

E1: Un des rares Valentines qui réussit à atteindre les lignes ennemies avant d'être mis hors de combat lors de l'anéantissement de la brigade ce jour. là. Le camouflage anglais apparait sous le camouflage de désert. Les unités de la 8th Armoured Division portait le motto divisionnel 'Go', bien qu'elle n'ait jamais combattu au complet. **E2:** Aucune autre indication que le nom, répété à l'arrière.

F1: Pendant les batailles de novembre 1941, le général de brigade Gatehouse dirigeait les opération assis sur une chaise-longue à l'arrière de son tank! Le losange représente le quartier-général. **F2:** Voir le commentaire en Anglais—il est impossible d'en donner la traduction faute de place. (1) = drapeau du chef de brigade. (2) = commandant de régiment. (3) = alternative, aux couleurs du régiment, le 4RTR. (4) = chef d'escadron, escadron 'B'. (5) = chef de peloton, 9ème peloton, escadron 'C'. (6) = alternative, peloton 1, escadron 'A'. (7) = peloton 8, escadron 'B', 8ème Hussards. (8) = 'Je suis hors de combat'. (9) = 'entrez en action'. (10) = 'Rassemblez-vous'. (11) = 'avancez'.

G1: Code-radio dans un cercle sur la tourelle, escadron 'C'; le petit cochon est la marque distinctive de ce tank. **G2:** tank personnel du général Montgomery à Alamein et plus tard; insigne de la 8ème armée avec 'Monty' peint à l'avant. Le drapeau du chef d'armée est rouge et noir.

H1: Identifications rudimentaires sur un tank neuf—la cocarde de la RAF etait probablement placée à l'arrière. **H2:** Ce tank a été utilisé par trois rériments à la suite, d'où l'identification confuse.

Farbtafeln

A1: Die weisse Nummer auf rotem Quadrat lässt das Regiment innerhalb einer Brigade erkennen; eine weisse Scheibe auf rot identifiziert die Division—die jerboa wurde in ein paar Wochen später hinzugefügt. Blaue Scheibe = 'C' Kompanie; alle Panzer dieses Regiments hatten Namen, die mit dem Buchstaben 'A' anfingen. **A2:** Neue 'Caunter-camouflage'; und endgültige Form des Divisionsabzeichens, mit jerboa. (Eingesetzt) Die Art des Kompanieabzeichens und Zugnummer, von den 8. Husaren benutzt, dessen Einheits-Seriennummer '25' war.

B1: Neu ausgestattet als Führungspanzer, dieser A9 hat noch seine Markierungen von der 'A' Kompanie, nunmehr veraltet. Brigadekommandeur Willison lässt den Erkennungswimpel in den Brigadefarben und den Wimpel, der die Tagesposition anzeigt über seine Kommandofahne in den RTR Farben mit einem Damenstrumpf. **B2:** Keine Markierungen werden getragen; die Caunter Tarnung ist deutlich zu sehen.

C1: Das Divisionsabzeichen war der Helm eines Ritters; die '40' lässt das Divisions Hauptquartier erkennen; und 'Evelyn' ist der individuelle Panzername. **C2:** Das Nashornabzeichen der Division und die Code-Nummer des Regiments waren in umgekehrter Position auf dem hinteren Rumpf wiederholt. Kompanieabzeichen und Namen waren in diesem Regiment in blau gehalten. **C3:** Ersatzpanser, dessen ursprüngliches Divisionsabzeichen ausgelöscht ist. Die '401' ist dessen Platz in der Formation durch die Minenfeldlücke.

D1: Alle 4 RTR Panzer hatten Namen, die mit 'D' und die 7 RTR, mit 'G' begannen. Die blauen Wimpel und die rot und weiss gemalten Streifen waren Erkennungszeichen für die Operation 'Crusader'. **D2:** Ein Held des hoffnungslosen Kampfes mit angeschlagenen Panzern bei Sidi Azeiz, 25. Nov. 1941; die Panzernamen der 42 RTR begannen mit 'P', und manche trugen das Brigadenabzeichen und die Regimentsnummer, wie hier: '173'.

E1: Einer der wenigen Valentines, die die Feindeslinien vor der Zerstörung an diesem Tag, an dem die Brigade vernichtet wurde, erreichten. Das englische Farbenschema scheint durch den neuen Wüstenfarbanstrich. Das 'Go' Abzeichen der 8th Armoured Division wurde getragen, obwohl sie niemals als eine zusammengefügte Division Kämpfte. **E2:** Ausser dem Namen, der am hinteren Rumpf wiederholt wurde, kein Abzeichen.

F1: Brigadekommandeur Gatehouse kommandierte von einem Liegestuhl hinten auf einem Panzer in den Schlachten vom Nov. 1941. Die Rautenform lässt das Hauptquartier erkennen. **F2:** Siehe den Kommentar in englischer Sprache—Platzmangel verbietet eine Übersetzung. (1) = Fahne des Brigadekommandeurs (2) = Regimentskommandeur (3) = Alternative, in den Regimentsfarben, 4 RTR (4) = Kompaniekommandeur, 'B' Kompanie (5) = Zugkommandeur, 9. Zug, 'C' Kompanie (6) = Alternative, 1 Zug, 'A' Kompanie (7) = 8 Zug, 'B' Kompanie, 8. Husaren (8) = 'Ich bin kamfunfähige' (9) = 'Nehmt teil am Kampf (10) = 'Sammeln' (11) = 'Vorwärts, marsch'.

G1: Radio-Rufzeichen im Kreis der 'C' Kompanie am Turm; die Schweinchenfigur ist die individuelle Panzerabzeichen. **G2:** Der persönliche Panzer von General Montgomery bei Alamein und nachher; das Abzeichen der 8. Armee und 'Monty' vorne aufgemalt, die Fahne des Armeekommandeurs in rot und schwarz.

H1: Einfache Markierungen auf neuem Panzer—das RAF Abzeichen war wahrscheinlich auf dem hinteren Deck markiert. **H2:** Dieser Panzer wurde von drei Regimentern in kurzer Reihenfolge benutzt, deshalb die verwirrten Abzeichen.